AMERICANS IN FRANCE

(LES AMÉRICAINS CHEZ NOUS)

Eugène Brieux

translated by

Felicia Hardison Londré

BROADWAY PLAY PUBLISHING INC
New York
www.broadwayplaypublishing.com
info@broadwayplaypublishing.com

AMERICANS IN FRANCE
© Copyright 2024 Felicia Hardison Londré

All rights reserved. This work is fully protected under the copyright laws of the United States of America. No part of this publication may be photocopied, reproduced, stored in a retrieval system, or transmitted, in any form or by any means, electronic, mechanical, recording, or otherwise, without the prior permission of the publisher. Additional copies of this play are available from the publisher.

Written permission is required for live performance of any sort. This includes readings, cuttings, scenes, and excerpts. For amateur and stock performances, please contact Broadway Play Publishing Inc. For all other rights please contact the translator c/o BPPI.

Cover art compliments of the Brian Stewart Collection

First edition: August 2024
I S B N: 979-8-88856-018-1

Book design: Marie Donovan
Page make-up: Adobe InDesign
Typeface: Palatino

LES AMÉRICAINS CHEZ NOUS was performed for the first time on 9 January 1920 at the Théâtre de l'Odéon in Paris.

THE AMERICANS IN FRANCE, an uncredited English version by A I du P Coleman, opened on 3 August 1920 at the Comedy Theatre in New York.

INTRODUCTION

It's always fascinating to see ourselves as others see us. In a 1988 Paris production of David Mamet's GLENGARRY GLEN ROSS, I was somewhat taken aback by the exaggerated machismo in the French actors' portrayals of those hard-boiled Chicago real estate men. They quaffed lemonade from a cooler on the filing cabinet and crushed the disposable cups in mighty hands. There is something of that French idea of American masculinity in Eugène Brieux's 1920 comedy *LES AMÉRICAINS CHEZ NOUS*. The exuberant character of the American Captain Smith, having fought for France during the Great War (1914-18), shows his can-do Yankee ingenuity in a civilian setting: how to repair a broken window when there is no glass to be found in the post-war market. And he whistles while he works! Similarly, the American nurse Nellie just happens to have a sewing kit in her handbag for an emergency dress repair. In her goal-oriented assertiveness, she prefigures the newly-enfranchised American woman of the 1920s.

With his sympathetic portrayal of Americans, Eugène Brieux (1858-1932) hoped that *LES AMÉRICAINS CHEZ NOUS* would contribute toward re-establishing the good will of the war years that was all too soon undermined by post-war financial hardships. He dedicated *LES AMÉRICAINS CHEZ NOUS* "To the women of the United States who tended us in our misery. Humble and respectful homage of gratitude from a Frenchman." Brieux felt a profound sense of gratitude for the untold thousands who knitted socks and made baby clothes at home even before the USA joined the Allies in April 1917 and for those who served abroad in canteens as "donut girls" and in telephone exchanges as "hello girls" and as nurses near the front lines.

While the roles and strengths of women, both American and French, during the Great War are sympathetically evoked in this post-war comedy, it also touches upon other issues that remain relevant to us. For example: How do people rebuild after a war? Should they try to reconstruct what was there before and recapture its memories? Or start afresh and experiment with something new? How much do we owe our long-ago ancestors? Or is respect for tradition a stranglehold? Should personal relationships ever be subject to measures of giving and receiving? What if we have to choose between beauty and utility? Between love and duty?

Brieux wrote the play at a difficult moment in post-World War I relations between France and the USA. These two Allied nations had been "best friends" since the time of George Washington and the Marquis de Lafayette. But when different cultures interact on a grand scale, there will always be misunderstandings as well as beneficial cross-influences. Above all, the play affirms the need to combat misunderstandings that arise from national, cultural, political, and other differences.

I am grateful to Professor Greer Gerni of the University of Missouri-Kansas City Conservatory's Theatre Division for championing the play and testing the translation in a rehearsed reading on 11 April 2024. The reading showed me where to trim and polish the

text, and it delighted me with the audience's warm, spontaneous laughter.
—**Felicia Hardison Londré**

CHARACTERS & SETTING

CAPTAIN GEORGE SMITH, *an American officer**
MONSIEUR CHARVET, *a landowner*
HENRI CHARVET, *his son, a doctor*
MONSIEUR RINGEAU, *a notary*
PIERRE BONAIN, *a mechanic*
MONSIEUR REMONTIER, *a landowner*
HENRIETTE CHARVET, HENRI'*s older sister*
NELLIE BROWN, *American Red Cross nurse*
MARIE BONAIN, PIERRE'*s sister*
APPOLONIE, *domestic servant of the* CHARVET *family*
LITTLE ETIENNE BONAIN, MARIE'*s little brother*
A Worker

**Brieux does not specify a rank in the original French.*

The action takes place at the CHARVET *home in Burgundy from April to September 1919.*

This play is dedicated
TO THE WOMEN OF THE UNITED STATES
who tended us in our misery

Humble and respectful homage
of gratitude from a Frenchman

Brieux

ACT ONE

(A grand but somewhat shabby salon in a chateau in Burgundy. It is morning, April 1919.)

*(*HENRIETTE *and* APPOLONIE *are on stage.* HENRIETTE *is 32, not unattractive, but tending to carelessness about her appearance. Her hair is pulled back and she dresses very simply.* APPOLONIE, *60s, wears an old-fashioned servant's dress. She speaks familiarly and forthrightly.* APPOLONIE *holds some pillows and is heading toward the door on the Right.)*

APPOLONIE: It's those Americans, I tell you—

HENRIETTE: *(Smiling)* Oh, now, Appolonie…

APPOLONIE: So. Mademoiselle doesn't see what they're up to? Ever since the Americans came, it's all crazy!

HENRIETTE: Of course, they have their own ways.

APPOLONIE: For one thing, why don't they talk like us? *(Trying to imitate them)* It's like *rrra-ah-ah-aah-oooh… rrrr…krik-krik…rrrrr…* Is that any way people with money should talk?

HENRIETTE: People with money?

APPOLONIE: The Americans. They're all millionaires.

HENRIETTE: You think so?

APPOLONIE: We think so because it's true. Just look at what they pay us for eggs. You know, mademoiselle, my sister sells in the market and she can tell you. For months and months, never once have we heard them say "that costs too much." Oh-ho, they've got money to burn. They all have gold mines in their gardens. Now, only yesterday… There's a restaurant in Dijon that buys up everything my sister has, only they didn't get it packed up quick enough. So along comes this American in a truck, and *krrr…krrr… ah-ah-aah-oooh…* He offers double. Then off he goes in a cloud of dust. With every last egg!

HENRIETTE: Enough of that! Here, take this pillow for Monsieur Henri's room and put those others in the yellow room. Tell me, Appolonie, do you think Monsieur Henri has changed?

APPOLONIE: Monsieur Henri! Now he's talking like the Yanks.

HENRIETTE: Fine, run along.

APPOLONIE: I heard Monsieur Henri with one of them: *krik-krik…rrra-ah-ah-aah-oooh…rrrr.*

HENRIETTE: That's not what I mean. Do you think he seems all right? *(Without waiting for a reply)* Of, course, he's exhausted. He was snoring enough to shake the house last night. But look—it's nine-thirty already and we haven't heard him get up yet.

APPOLONIE: Oh, he flew the coop quite some time ago.

HENRIETTE: He went out already?

APPOLONIE: He did.

HENRIETTE: You're sure? He was fast asleep when I carried in his *café au lait*. Did you check with him whether he needed anything?

APPOLONIE: He would call me if he did. Like, last night he wanted the oil lamp at ten o'clock.

HENRIETTE: I gave him a very short candle so he wouldn't stay up. Did you take him the lamp?

APPOLONIE: Well, I tried to tell him it was too late for lamplight. But he—

HENRIETTE: What did he say?

APPOLONIE: He said he's twenty-six years old and he fought in the war and he knows when he wants a lamp.

HENRIETTE: So true. The poor boy. But still… Did you take him the *Gazette*?

APPOLONIE: He didn't want it. He asked for the *Progressive*.

HENRIETTE: *The Progressive*!!! Oh, but here he is now. You can run along.

(*Enter* HENRI, *looking very young.*)

HENRIETTE: Good morning, Henri. You're in civilian clothes?

HENRI: As you see.

(HENRI *crosses to open the door for* APPOLONIE *who has her arms full of pillows.*)

HENRI: Polonie, you are like a hen with thirty-six ducklings.

APPOLONIE: Thank you, Monsieur Henri. (*She exits.*)

HENRIETTE: The pillows are for you.

HENRI: (*Indifferently*) Ah.

HENRIETTE: Always before, you could never have enough pillows.

HENRI: Always before. That was then.

HENRIETTE: But these civilian clothes. Where did you find them?

HENRI: I looked where they were "always before". In the armoire. Am I a clever boy?

HENRIETTE: Luckily I got them all ready for you last Monday. And where did you go this early?

HENRI: To see a friend.

HENRIETTE: You pay calls before ten in the morning now!? Was your friend out of bed?

HENRI: Yes, he's been operating his machine since dawn. I went to see Pierre Bonain at the farm. We hadn't seen each other since the time… well, the time we were under fire together. And there were some of the other guys too. It was great.

HENRIETTE: Now I'm jealous of Pierre Bonain. You didn't stop to say good morning to me.

HENRI: *(Very affectionately and cheerfully)* Good morning, big sis!

(HENRI *hugs* HENRIETTE.)

HENRIETTE: So happy to have you home, little brother. You—going off to see friends instead of talking with me!

HENRI: We had all day yesterday—you and me and Father.

HENRIETTE: You must have so many stories to tell.

HENRI: *(Evasively)* Bah!

HENRIETTE: No?

HENRI: Oh, yes, we have stories. But we're not ready to talk about…all that. I'd much rather hear about home. Father seems different.

HENRIETTE: Older?

HENRI: No. Different. *(A beat)* Or maybe I'm different.

HENRIETTE: Older.

HENRI: What about his big project? His book on the parliamentary history of Dijon?

HENRIETTE: He couldn't focus on it during the war. But he finally mentioned it yesterday—as if ready to get back to it.

(HENRI, *seeing* CAPTAIN SMITH *in his US Army uniform, outside the French doors:*)

HENRI: Look! Here's an American paying us a call.

HENRIETTE: Already? He's early then.

HENRI: You know him?

HENRIETTE: Yes, he's the one who bought the Oak Woods for the American army. But Father isn't ready yet. *(She rings.)* I don't want to keep him company. He speaks French, but I never know what to say to him. Let's go for a stroll down to the pond.

(To APPOLONIE, *who enters)*

HENRIETTE: There's Captain Smith. Please ask him to wait here. Give him these newspapers. *(To* HENRI*)* Will you come with me?

(HENRI *takes a few steps with her*)

HENRI: Yes. But this Captain Smith, does he work at the hospital?

HENRIETTE: No, my dear Doctor Henri Charvet, he doesn't. He's not one of your colleagues.

HENRI: Still I'd like to ask him something.

HENRIETTE: Can't it wait?

HENRI: Give me just a moment with him.

HENRIETTE: I'll be in the front hall.

(HENRIETTE *exits.* APPOLONIE *re-enters almost immediately, ushering in* SMITH, *who wears a United States Army officer's uniform. Late 30s or so, youngish, manly, heartily straightforward, sympathetic.*)

APPOLONIE: Come in, monsieur. Monsieur Charvet said your appointment is at ten. You are early. *(She finds something to busy herself while she regards him with curiosity)*

SMITH: Early bird catches… Yes, I'm early.

HENRI: Captain Smith, permit me to introduce myself. I am Henri Charvet, adjutant in the French Army medical service. I think you've met my sister Henriette. But there's something I'd like to ask you.

SMITH: Fire away.

HENRI: Have you heard of any new staff expected at our little nearby hospital?

SMITH: Two surgeons are coming—with their support staff.

HENRI: The ones who were at Rheims? Doctor Martson… ?

SMITH: I think so.

HENRI: With his staff?

SMITH: Yes, nurses.

HENRI: Nurses. Good. Thank you, monsieur, thank you very much. *(Exiting right, to* APPOLONIE*)* Polonie, tell my sister that I need to… Oh, tell her whatever you like, but she shouldn't wait for me. *(To* SMITH*)* Thank you, Monsieur. *(He exits.)*

APPOLONIE: Well… *(She goes out the other door, grimacing behind* SMITH*'s back)*

SMITH: *(Distractedly flips through a newspaper; reading)* "Franco-American sky clouds over…" "Paris Peace Conference proceeds at glacial pace…"

*(*ETIENNE *enters through an interior door. He is a little peasant, about twelve years old, properly dressed, open and cheerful. He runs to the table to take a book.)*

SMITH: Hey there, hi! My friend from… We met in front of the school!

ETIENNE: *(Happily surprised)* It's you—the American monsieur! *(He runs to* SMITH*)*

SMITH: *(Picking him up and holding him high)* What do you say to an American?

ETIENNE: "Hi, hi, howdy do?" *(He laughs uproariously)*

SMITH: And what else?

ETIENNE: "Hurrah for the USA!"

SMITH: And I say "Vive la France!" *(Putting him down)* You are a jolly good little fellow! So you remember me?

ETIENNE: Yes, monsieur.

SMITH: "Monsieur!" Didn't you learn two days ago to call me Captain George? We're old friends, aren't we?

ETIENNE: *(Laughing)* You're tickling me!

SMITH: Of course, since we know each other so well.

ETIENNE: Since Thursday.

SMITH: See, we're old friends! Do you ever play kickball?

ETIENNE: I practice in the street. And I have a ball. *(He starts to take a ball out of his pocket.)*

SMITH: Do you think you're as strong as I am?

ETIENNE: Yes, I am strong.

SMITH: Do you live here?

ETIENNE: No, I just came to get this book I left here.

SMITH: Do you know Mademoiselle Charvet?

ETIENNE: Yes, I do know Mademoiselle Henriette. She's teaching me to…

SMITH: What?

ETIENNE: Read and everything. Monsieur Henri came home yesterday.

SMITH: Who is Monsieur Henri?

ETIENNE: Mademoiselle Henriette's brother! Don't you know?

(ETIENNE *tries to cram the book into his pocket, but his ball falls out.* SMITH *pushes it back with his foot.* ETIENNE *picks it up as* SMITH *pretends to tackle him for it.* ETIENNE *tosses it away from* SMITH—*and breaks a glass pane in the door.)*

ETIENNE: Oh, no!

SMITH: That's not how we play ball.

ETIENNE: *(Agonized)* It's broken! …Oh! …Captain George, does that window cost a lot?

(HENRIETTE *enters.)*

HENRIETTE: *(To* SMITH *with a sign of greeting)* My father is on his way, monsieur. *(To* ETIENNE*)* Etienne, are you entertaining Captain Smith?

ETIENNE: *(Fighting tears)* Mademoiselle…

SMITH: Excuse me, mademoiselle. I wanted to show my friend Etienne how we play ball and I broke that window.

ETIENNE: No, Mademoiselle Henriette, I did it. Please don't tell my "little mother." Don't tell her. Please.

HENRIETTE: Such mischief! You know we can't get any window glass these days. But I won't trouble her with it. Run along now.

(ETIENNE, *embarrassed, takes his book and turns to go.)*

SMITH: Goodbye, "sir".

ETIENNE: *(Weeping)* Goodbye, my…American monsieur.

SMITH: See you Thursday, in front of the school. No windowpanes there!

(ETIENNE *shakes his head sadly and exits.*)

HENRIETTE: Poor little fellow! It's not his fault he craves attention. There are nine of them in his house.

(SMITH *has taken a notebook from his pocket and is measuring the broken pane.*)

HENRIETTE: What are you doing?

SMITH: So I can replace your window.

HENRIETTE: You can go all the way to Dijon and you won't find anything. We can be glad winter is over.

SMITH: We'll see… Is Etienne really afraid of his… what did he call her?… "little mother"?

HENRIETTE: His "little mother" is his sister, Marie Bonain. She raised him. Oh, here's my father.

(*Enter* MONSIEUR CHARVET, *age sixty, charismatic.*)

CHARVET: (*Shaking hands with* SMITH) Forgive me, Captain Smith, for keeping you waiting. Please sit down. Monsieur Ringeau surely will be here soon. At ten.

SMITH: I should apologize for coming early. It's just that I wanted a moment with you on a different matter.

CHARVET: (*With just a touch of anxiety*) Is there some problem with our arrangements for the sale of the Oak Woods?

SMITH: Not at all. In fact, just yesterday, I left a check for fifty thousand francs with your banker in Dijon.

CHARVET: Our contract—the private agreement we signed—is binding. Our meeting today to sign in front of the notary is purely a formality and I'm sorry to have to impose this extra step on you.

SMITH: Hey, we're copacetic! But what I do want to ask you… Okay, now I am not speaking as a representative of the United States Army. Now I'm speaking just for myself and two friends. You own quite a bit of land here…

CHARVET: *(Smiling)* Let me stop you right there. Are you looking to purchase land?

SMITH: Yes.

CHARVET: *(Unruffled, with perfect urbanity)* My family estate is only a small parcel of what it once was. It used to be a vast property that the king, Henri IV, awarded to Pierre Jeannin, the first president of the parliament of Dijon, my esteemed ancestor. Jeannin's descendants—almost all—were magistrates. They were born here and died here. In short, this remaining property is not for sale. And since I am speaking with an American, I must add: Not at any price.

SMITH: I sort of expected that. Yes, I knew this chateau was here already before my country even existed. And that's something I admire more than you can guess. I understand your refusal. I accept it. So I'll propose instead a partnership.

CHARVET: A partnership?

SMITH: Yes. One that will increase the value of your property.

CHARVET: Its value has withstood the centuries.

SMITH: "Value" means something else to me.

CHARVET: We are happy with the way things are.

SMITH: Now there's the attitude that's holding France back.

CHARVET: Perhaps.

SMITH: Your income could increase tenfold.

CHARVET: *(Still courteous)* The same attitude that's holding France back tells me I have enough.

SMITH: Monsieur Charvet, I have total respect for you and your daughter. I would never want to throw a monkey wrench… Okay, the notary is going to arrive at any moment, so to make it short: Would you allow me to propose a plan involving your property? I would submit it to you as a project for your consideration. Absolutely no obligation on your part. If you don't like what I propose, you say so and that's it. You see, at present you have a lot of land by European standards and it's being used for nothing but sheep grazing.

CHARVET: It cannot be otherwise.

SMITH: It can! With irrigation. You have water.

CHARVET: I repeat: we are not interested in changing the way we do things. We have lived on these lands and allowed the farmers born on these farms to run them without us telling them what to do. They too have family heritages and I am not about to disrupt that.

SMITH: It's possible to make everyone happy. Just tell me I can go ahead and put together a proposal.

CHARVET: It's a waste of time.

SMITH: Even so. Suppose it is only a pipe dream. Just indulge me. In the name of Franco-American friendship.

CHARVET: *(Smiling)* You have a way of making it difficult to refuse. *(He thinks for a moment.)* Well, no harm in it. Now, I seem to remember somewhere in my papers an old document that might be useful to you. Yes, I could show it to you.

SMITH: When?

CHARVET: I'll have to search for it. One day soon.

SMITH: How about right now? As we've learned to say, "Toot sweet!"

CHARVET: *(Laughing)* Right now? *"Tout de suite?"* Well, come back later this morning.

SMITH: Thank you. And then soon I'll bring you a plan. For your amazing land. With the pond.

(MONSIEUR RINGEAU *enters. He is a bureaucrat, aware of his importance.)*

CHARVET: Monsieur Ringeau, you remember Captain Smith?

RINGEAU: Certainly. I've brought you the receipt from Monsieur Charvet's banker attesting to the deposit of the full amount that was agreed upon. *(He takes some stamped papers from his briefcase.)* Captain Smith, we haven't filled in your given names.

SMITH: George Robert Smith. But it's important to note that I merely act as a representative of the purchasing agency for the United States Army.

RINGEAU: Yes, that is noted. Your profession?

SMITH: Voluntarily enlisted in the United States Army—for the love of France. Wounded in the Meuse-Argonne. Before the war, I was production foreman in a factory.

(Seeing RINGEAU*'s look of surprise:)*

SMITH: Not all Americans are millionaires. But I do make about two thousand francs a month.

RINGEAU: Married, widowed, or bachelor?

SMITH: You need to know all that? Okay, bachelor.

RINGEAU: Bachelor. Date and place of birth?

SMITH: January 25, 1882, in Jefferson, Texas.

RINGEAU: Now Monsieur Alexandre Charvet, born…I have that. No profession.

SMITH: No profession? *(To* CHARVET*)* You let him put "no profession"? That's an insult.

CHARVET: *(Smiling)* You can say "landowner" if you like.

RINGEAU: *(Back to his documents)* And Mademoiselle Henriette Charvet. *(Gallantly)* I apologize, mademoiselle, I do have to enter your age.

HENRIETTE: Everyone knows I'm thirty-two.

RINGEAU: No one would believe it if you didn't say so.

SMITH: *(Good-naturedly naïve)* This whole process is so strange. Monsieur Ringeau, do all French notaries have to jump through these hoops into the red tape?

(Everyone laughs.)

RINGEAU: We make allowances for foreigners. So back to the business at hand. *(He reads very rapidly and incomprehensibly a long passage from the legal document.)*

SMITH: Slow down. I'm not following.

RINGEAU: You don't need to understand it.

SMITH: Then why do you read it to us?

RINGEAU: It's the custom.

SMITH: Do you ever wish you could change the custom?

RINGEAU: *(A bit put off)* This is how we do it.

HENRIETTE: Pardon me, monsieur. *(Smiling, to* SMITH*)* We do have these ancient practices… *(To* RINGEAU*)* Please continue.

RINGEAU: "With all his legal rights, titles, and appurtenances…"

SMITH: Say that again?

RINGEAU: "With all his legal rights, titles, and appurtenances…"

SMITH: His "titles"?

RINGEAU: Yes, titles and appurtenances. It's the same thing.

SMITH: Then why the repetition?

RINGEAU: It's our custom.

SMITH: I don't get it.

RINGEAU: It doesn't matter. But if you stop me after every word, we'll never finish. *(Returning to his document)* "Brings and carries with it…"

SMITH: Pardon me. Brings what?

RINGEAU: The property.

SMITH: The woods?

RINGEAU: Yes.

SMITH: The woods bring and carry with it the woods!?!?

CHARVET: It's just a legal formulation.

SMITH: *(Impatient)* But look here. We already put it down on paper: Mademoiselle Charvet sells to the United States Army, represented by Captain George Smith, the woods known as Oak Woods, for such and such sum. Is that a legal formulation?

RINGEAU: Indeed. Under Roman law it's what we call *l'actio venditi.*

SMITH: If it's not clear in French, it certainly won't help to put it in Latin. Is what we already put down on paper a legal transaction or not?

RINGEAU: This is a deed…

SMITH: This isn't a deed. It's gobbledygook! Is my paper valid?

RINGEAU: Of course it is, but this makes it even more valid.

SMITH: It's got to be either valid or not valid.

RINGEAU: It's valid, but…

HENRIETTE & CHARVET: Messieurs! …Messieurs!

RINGEAU: This is what a notary does. It's the custom.

SMITH: Payment built in for useless services!

RINGEAU: *(Gathering his papers)* Monsieur, my dignity as a representative of the ministry forbids me to continue in this vein.

SMITH: And my dignity as an honest man forbids me to sign what I don't understand.

RINGEAU: I beg your forgiveness, Monsieur Charvet, but you realize that there are limits to one's patience! Even a notary's.

CHARVET: *(To* RINGEAU*)* Please, give us just a moment. *(To* SMITH, *well-meaning but very pronounced)* Captain Smith, as a practical man, you must see that it's no use revolting against customs and traditions that cannot be changed? By reading this deed to us, the notary is merely doing his duty. The formalities that you find irritating are ones of ancient standing, which we French find acceptable. If you want to do business in France, it's probably a good idea to go along with French ways of doing it. *(With a smile)* You are here as a friend, not as a reformer.

SMITH: *(After a moment's reflection)* You are right. We Yanks are still wet behind the ears, but we mean well. You have convinced me and I've learned from it. *(To* RINGEAU*)* Monsieur Ringeau, with your indulgence, I'll stop by your office and figure it all out so we're both satisfied. Why don't I just go along with you right now? Goodbye, mademoiselle. Monsieur Charvet, I'll stop back here in a little while to look at the document you mentioned.

RINGEAU: *(To* CHARVET*)* Does that meet your approval?

CHARVET: Yes, certainly.

RINGEAU: *(Giving him a paper)* And here is your bank statement showing the deposit.

CHARVET: Thank you.

SMITH: Let's go, Monsieur Ringeau. You and me, we'll translate that document into some French lingo that anyone can understand. *(Clapping him on the shoulder)*

RINGEAU: Ouch!

SMITH: We're friends now.

(SMITH *and* RINGEAU *exit.*)

CHARVET: *(Studies the papers that* RINGEAU *left with him; melancholy)* This is all I have to leave you, my sweet child.

HENRIETTE: I'm satisfied, Father.

CHARVET: But it's your dowry.

HENRIETTE: Marriage is not for everyone.

CHARVET: I want your happiness.

HENRIETTE: My happiness is seeing Henri settled.

CHARVET: The great regret of my old age is not being able to provide better for you.

HENRIETTE: We have done the best we could. It's not your fault. Let's keep our eyes on the future. Our Henri.

CHARVET: *(Still looking at his paper)* Yes… For the future. We need to have a frank conversation with the Rémontiers.

(HENRI *enters.*)

CHARVET: Henri, don't make any plans for this afternoon or tomorrow. You and I must pay some calls together.

HENRI: Very well, Father.

CHARVET: *(As he exits)* We'll call upon the Rémontiers today. But first I'll telephone to be certain they aren't in Paris. Be ready soon.

HENRI: I'll be ready.

HENRIETTE: Where have you been?

HENRI: At the American hospital.

HENRIETTE: Let's sit down. We need to talk about your future.

HENRI: *(Gaily)* Oh, that's too serious. My future is not in a hurry.

HENRIETTE: Yes, it is. Doctor Bréançon is planning to sell his practice by the end of the year. He will hold it for you, but he wants a contract.

HENRI: You know I still have to defend my thesis.

HENRIETTE: By the way, I found some materials for your thesis. I put them on the table. Did you see them?

HENRI: Yes. Very interesting. Sorry I've neglected to thank you. Where did you unearth those things?

HENRIETTE: I asked a researcher in Paris.

HENRI: You should have been the man of the family.

HENRIETTE: *(Feigning off-handedness)* There is a way that everything can work out: if you would marry the little Rémontier girl.

HENRI: Mathilde?

HENRIETTE: I don't see any objections coming from their side. She's a sweetheart, and you are good friends with her.

HENRI: Friends. Like comrades. But not—

HENRIETTE: *(Very tender, very persuasive)* Listen, Henri. If you would marry Mathilde, you'll get a charming wife and a dowry. Not a huge amount, but enough. You can marry her as soon as you've defended your thesis. Then a month-long honeymoon… Italy maybe… no Switzerland, since they were neutral. Then you settle in here and accompany the doctor on his visits. Once he retires, you will be very nicely situated.

HENRI: You've planned my life.

HENRIETTE: Haven't I always done that? Ever since Mother died. And look at you now. When you have children, I'll be the happiest aunt. I want to start planning their educations.

(CHARVET *enters with some papers.*)

CHARVET: There. I've found the estate map for Captain Smith, though I don't think it will be much use to him. It's older and more fragile than I remembered, so he will have to look at it here. It's the original copy.

HENRIETTE: I will tell him.

(CHARVET *exits.*)

HENRIETTE: *(To* HENRI*)* Well?

HENRI: It's a lot to think about.

HENRIETTE: Do think fast, little brother. Don't let this opportunity slip away.

HENRI: Contracting with Bréançon could cost—no, I can't accept more of your sacrifices.

HENRIETTE: Sacrifices? It's for my own happiness too.

HENRI: But you…

HENRIETTE: Then let me say it plain and simple: supporting you is my happiness.

HENRI: *(Affectionately)* Already I owe you so much.

HENRIETTE: You owe me nothing. Or if we tallied our balance sheets, I would come out in your debt. You have given the meaning to my life. Let yourself be loved, that's all I ask.

HENRI: You've been my mother and my friend.

HENRIETTE: No brother and sister could be closer than us. All those years we depended on each other! We thought alike. We were soul-mates!

HENRI: You were my guiding spirit.

HENRIETTE: After Mother passed away, we were like children lost in the woods. Without you, how would I have found home? Everything I did for you came back to enrich my own soul.

HENRI: Yes. But Henriette…

HENRIETTE: It's so nice to remember those bonds now. There was never enough time when you came home on leave.

HENRI: My leaves were always so short.

HENRIETTE: And you didn't write home very much. Oh, how I yearned for your letters!

HENRI: It was wrong of me not to write more often. But now it's in the past, isn't it?

HENRIETTE: Yes, in the past. And now you're here in the present! Next comes the future. Your marriage.

HENRI: As I said, I need some time. Oh, here's Captain Smith.

(APPOLONIE *ushers* SMITH *in.*)

HENRIETTE: Captain Smith, here's the map you wanted to see. But my father asks that you not take it.

SMITH: Of course. (*He glances at it.*) 1825. It's fragile, so I won't even pick it up.

HENRIETTE: Shall I leave you to study it?

SMITH: Please, don't let me inconvenience you.

(HENRI *exits, and we hear greetings.* HENRIETTE *is about to exit when* MARIE BONAIN *enters. She is 23, very simply dressed in black, no hat.*)

HENRIETTE: *(To* SMITH*)* Let me introduce Marie Bonain. She's the "little mother" of your friend Etienne. *(To* MARIE*)* What is it, Marie? You may speak in front of Captain Smith.

MARIE: Mademoiselle Henriette, I've come to beg pardon for the window that my brother broke. As soon as you know how much it costs, please tell me. Etienne has his own little box of coins—

SMITH: Mademoiselle Bonain, I'm the one who is going to replace the windowpane, and I will tell you.

MARIE: That is very kind of you, sir. It's important for children to take responsibility. *Au revoir,* mademoiselle. Goodbye, Monsieur Captain. *(She crosses to the door.)*

SMITH: That tiny little thing, is she the one who raised her seven brothers and sisters?

HENRIETTE: It's remarkable, isn't it? *(She crosses to the door and calls.)* Marie…

(HENRIETTE *brings* MARIE *over to* SMITH.*)*

HENRIETTE: Marie, tell Captain Smith your story.

MARIE: *(Perplexed)* My story?

HENRIETTE: During the war.

MARIE: My story during the war? But you know quite well, Mademoiselle Henriette.

HENRIETTE: Captain Smith has not heard it.

MARIE: Well, we worked our farm.

HENRIETTE: And what else?

MARIE: Well, that's all.

HENRIETTE: *(To* SMITH*)* Her mother died when little Louise was born. *(To* MARIE*)* What year was that?

MARIE: In 1910.

HENRIETTE: How old were you?

MARIE: I was thirteen.

HENRIETTE: And who took care of your baby sister Louise?

MARIE: I did, of course. Mademoiselle Henriette, it's strange to talk about this.

HENRIETTE: And your father died two years later. And because of that, when war was declared… Come on, do tell it!

MARIE: I don't know…

HENRIETTE: Who worked your land?

MARIE: We all did.

HENRIETTE: All who?

MARIE: My brothers and then me, everyone who was big enough.

HENRIETTE: How many brothers were drafted?

MARIE: Five: Pierre, François, Antoine, Henri, and Emile.

HENRIETTE: How many came home?

MARIE: Three.

HENRIETTE: So in August 1914, who was left on your farm?

MARIE: Me. But I was nineteen by then. And then George was sixteen and Joseph was thirteen. And there was little Etienne. And our baby sister Louise.

SMITH: What did you do?

MARIE: What else! The same as our parents did. We worked the land.

SMITH: Just you and your little brothers?

MARIE: When it got tough, the neighbors would help out.

HENRIETTE: What did you send your brothers at the front?

MARIE: There wasn't much. We knitted things. And sent some bacon!

HENRIETTE: I used to see some light in your windows very late at night. What were you doing then?

MARIE: Oh, we always had mending to do. You know, socks, they wear out. And seats of pants.

SMITH: Those must have been hard times. Did you ever think of just chucking it all?

MARIE: Chucking it? You mean giving up? You are joking, of course. Monsieur Captain, around here everyone knows, going back from grandfather to grandfather, it's the Bonains who made the land give back.

HENRIETTE: Marie, you are truly a brave girl.

SMITH: Where do you live, Marie?

MARIE: *(Pointing)* Over there.

HENRIETTE: It's the first farmhouse you see when you leave here.

MARIE: *Au revoir*, Mademoiselle Henriette. Good day, Monsieur Captain.

HENRIETTE: She's not like the French women in the novels you Americans read, is she? That's why I wanted to introduce her to you. Well, now… Your map is there, on the table.

SMITH: *(Focusing on the map, then a shout of excitement)* Yes!

HENRIETTE: Pardon?

SMITH: Oh, just thinking out loud.

HENRIETTE: I'll see you later, Captain Smith.

SMITH: *(To himself)* Yes! *(He glances again at the map.)* 1825! Hard for me to imagine.

(Lights change to indicate passage of time. SMITH exits during the dimming of lights. Lights up, SMITH re-enters and places on the table a pane of glass wrapped in paper, then a small hammer and some putty. He unwraps the glass and checks it against the broken pane. He removes his military jacket to get to work, whistling as he works. He takes the tools and steps into the next room to fit the glass from the other side. While SMITH is out of sight, APPOLONIE ushers MONSIEUR REMONTIER into the room.

APPOLONIE: I will tell Monsieur Charvet and Mademoiselle Henriette that you are here.

(APPOLONIE exits. SMITH re-enters without seeing REMONTIER. He hammers while whistling loudly. REMONTIER becomes visibly annoyed and finally explodes.)

REMONTIER: Tell me, how long do you plan to continue that whistling?

SMITH: Oh, hello! Sorry. I do it without thinking— whistle while I work!

REMONTIER: So you're not from around here?

SMITH: Nope.

REMONTIER: Evidently. If you knew who I am, you would not answer me that way. And who are you?

SMITH: For this job, I'm a glazier. And you are—?

REMONTIER: I am Monsieur Rémontier. Landowner.

SMITH: My compliments. (*Surveying the installed pane of glass*) That should do it. (*He puts his jacket on.*)

REMONTIER: (*Seeing the ribbons and the Cross of Valor*) Ah!… I beg your pardon.

(HENRIETTE *enters.*)

HENRIETTE: (*To* REMONTIER) Bonjour, Monsieur Rémontier.

SMITH: Your window is as good as new!

HENRIETTE: How…? You…?

SMITH: You were absolutely right. There is no window glass available from here to Dijon. (*Laughing*) But I had a glass window at my place, and I had a glass-cutter—

HENRIETTE: So now you have some fresh air at your place?

SMITH: Fresh April air! You French would say "the one who breaks the glass must pay for it." But I say "the one who busts a window must fix it."

(CHARVET *enters.*)

SMITH: Monsieur Charvet, thanks for finding that map. I see that you have a meeting, so I'll come back later to look at it more closely. So long for now.

(SMITH *exits.*)

REMONTIER: (*To* CHARVET, *shaking hands*) How are you? That's a very unusual glazier you have there.

CHARVET: (*To* HENRIETTE) Glazier?

HENRIETTE: (*Laughing*) Yes, Captain Smith wanted to replace the window glass he broke when he was playing in here with the little Bonain boy.

CHARVET: (*To* REMONTIER) And how is Madame Rémontier?

REMONTIER: She is very well, thank you.

HENRIETTE: She didn't come with you? And Mathilde?

REMONTIER: No, your father invited me to talk business.

HENRIETTE: Yes, of course. Henri and I will pay a call on them.

REMONTIER: We were so glad to hear that your brother has returned! Is Henri good health?

CHARVET: Excellent.

REMONTIER: I look forward to shaking the hero's hand. We saw him last time when he was on leave, you remember? Is he here?

CHARVET: Yes. But Henriette and I were hoping to talk with you… about Henri, but without him.

REMONTIER: As you wish.

(HENRIETTE, *giving* REMONTIER *a large envelope:*)

HENRIETTE: Monsieur Rémontier, you will find in this envelope the amount we owe you. It was tallied up by our notary in consultation with yours.

REMONTIER: You are very kind, mademoiselle, but I must insist again that I have absolutely no need for the money.

HENRIETTE: It's just that we do have a need to repay you.

REMONTIER: A need?

CHARVET: Yes. It will permit us to talk freely on a subject that concerns all of us.

HENRIETTE: It's about my brother.

CHARVET: We want to help him establish himself.

HENRIETTE: And we thought that maybe Mathilde…

CHARVET: But I beg you to hear me out before you reply. You need to know…

REMONTIER: Willingly, my friend, and I can tell you already—

CHARVET: *(Stopping him)* Excuse me, I must continue. You see, for a long time now, even before the death of my dear wife, we have been ruined. I won't burden you with the circumstances, except to say that I am entirely at fault.

HENRIETTE: It was not your fault at all, Father. You were badly misled.

CHARVET: We subsist frugally on what our property brings in, after we pay the interest on the mortgage, which is very close to the actual value for which it's covered. Henri was able to continue his medical studies without knowing that it was thanks to his sister. As soon as she reached legal age, Henriette took a loan on the land her aunt had left her as a dowry. You were the lender, and that was the beginning of our good friendship.

HENRIETTE: Henri is on the verge of completing his medical degree, and it's true he has no material possessions to bring to a marriage. But he has a generous heart and the clean conscience of a man of integrity and the solid preparation to earn a living.

CHARVET: What Henriette says, I second with all my heart. We have been imagining that perhaps he and mademoiselle your daughter…

HENRIETTE: I must add that Henri knows nothing of all this.

CHARVET: It's just that our children always seemed to enjoy their times together.

HENRIETTE: And you need to know also that I've sold the Oak Woods, which was the security on your loan. So Henri has nothing to inherit from me.

CHARVET: Nor from me, nor from anyone else.

REMONTIER: My dear friends, have you finished? I would have spared you all these revelations. But perhaps it has given you some relief to air them…

CHARVET: I believe so. What about you, Henriette?

HENRIETTE: Yes, Father.

CHARVET: *(Overcome with emotion)* You've always been a perfect daughter. Your mother would have been proud of you.

REMONTIER: Yes, mademoiselle, your father is right. And you, sir… You know, you haven't really surprised me. On another day I would have been the one to come and seek your thoughts on a possible union of our children. But, of course, that is for Mathilde to decide.

CHARVET: While Henri too would…

HENRIETTE: First we wanted to learn from you whether his lack of inheritance would disqualify him.

REMONTIER: Your thoughtfulness is commendable. Mathilde's dowry should suffice for a young couple's basic needs.

HENRIETTE: We assume that Henri can take the place of Doctor Bréançon when he retires.

REMONTIER: Buying that client list will be the first item from Mathilde's dowry.

HENRIETTE: You have made me so happy.

REMONTIER: So there's nothing left to do except get the consent of the principals in the matter.

CHARVET: And to thank you with all our hearts.

REMONTIER: Until soon then.

CHARVET: Until soon!

(REMONTIER *exits.*)

HENRIETTE: Oh, Father, it's a happy day!

CHARVET: Let's wait till it's over. You know the old saying—

(HENRI *enters.*)

HENRIETTE: Did you see Monsieur Rémontier just now?

HENRI: No, I avoided him.

CHARVET: But why?

HENRI: Because I suspect—well, something Henriette said earlier—it seemed as if you might be considering a marriage for Mathilde and me.

HENRIETTE: You don't want to marry her?

HENRI: No…not exactly. Not now.

HENRIETTE: What's the point of waiting? Father said it a while ago: a young doctor has to be a married man. Isn't that so?

HENRI: Probably so.

HENRIETTE: What's going on with you? Are you hiding something from us?

HENRI: Of course not.

HENRIETTE: Come on. I know you too well. What is it?

HENRI: Nothing.

HENRIETTE: Something. Are you keeping secrets from me?

HENRI: No. Listen… Just listen to me and don't get upset. And try to understand.

HENRIETTE: Mon Dieu! Tell us! Oh, these four years of separation! Tell us what it is.

HENRI: I am no longer free to marry.

CHARVET: You have a fiancée!?!?

HENRI: A fiancée… Not exactly. But maybe…I met a young woman.

HENRIETTE: Do I know her?

HENRI: No.

CHARVET: Is she from around here?

HENRI: No.

CHARVET: How do you know her?

HENRI: We met at the hospital in Reims.

CHARVET: She's a nurse?

HENRI: Yes.

HENRIETTE: French, of course.

HENRI: American.

(Long pause)

HENRIETTE: How old is she?

HENRI: She's twenty-two.

HENRIETTE: A respectable young woman?

HENRI: A respectable young woman.

(A beat)

HENRIETTE: Is she still in Reims?

HENRI: No, she asked for a transfer. She's the one I went to see at the American hospital this morning. But they wouldn't let me in.

HENRIETTE: Are you engaged to her?

HENRI: Not exactly engaged, like that. But we love each other.

CHARVET: What about her parents?

HENRI: They're in the United States. In Chicago. Her father had a management position.

HENRIETTE: Are they wealthy?

HENRI: I don't know. I don't think so. No.

HENRIETTE: How long have you been in love?

HENRI: Six months.

HENRIETTE: *(Dismayed)* Mon Dieu! All my beautiful dreams for you!

HENRI: Henriette, please. Calm down. Listen.

CHARVET: *(To* HENRIETTE*)* Pull yourself together, my child.

HENRIETTE: *(Making an effort)* It's such a shock! All right, I'm calm. It was the shock.

HENRI: Oh, Father, she's such a pure and glorious young woman. She has such courage. She's so generous. For a year she's been tending our wounded. Before she came to France, she devoted herself to the poor of her own city. We served together in Reims. We both looked death in the eye under the bombardments. She saved lives when some of wounded might have… but she had the skill. Once we had to evacuate a ward that caught fire. If only you could have seen her: calm, strong.… And how she knows just what to say to fear…to grief. There was a child, a child who died in her arms. That was the day before we declared our feelings to each other. You'll see, Henriette, you will love her.

CHARVET: Have you resolved to marry her?

HENRI: Yes, Father.

CHARVET: My son, five years ago, even if you had been as old as you are now, if you had spoken to me then of marrying a foreigner, I would have forbidden it. But you have been in the war. For the last four years, you have lived alongside death. I feel as though I no longer have the right to assert my wishes over you as I would have done then. Everything has changed. Our hierarchy of values, as you were saying yesterday evening, is turned upside down. Our children have earned the respect of their elders. *(A beat)* It's true, we

were imagining our own idea of a beautiful future for
you....

HENRIETTE: Such a beautiful future.

CHARVET: But you put your life on the line, so you are
the master of it. We will receive this young woman into
our home...and... (*Overcome with emotion, he cannot
continue*)

HENRIETTE: Oh, little brother! my precious little
brother!

CHARVET: You understand that I must make inquiries
about her family, and correspond with her. I ask you
to wait two months, or perhaps three—while I pursue
the formalities. And I promise you, I will do nothing to
stretch out this waiting period.

HENRI: Thank you, Father. I will wait.

(APPOLONIE *enters.*)

APPOLONIE: There's an American nurse here who
wants to speak with Monsieur Henri. Here's her card.

(*Stunned looks from* CHARVET *and* HENRIETTE)

APPOLONIE: I had her wait in the small salon.

(HENRI *takes the card, embarrassed.*)

CHARVET: Is it your friend?

HENRI: (*A bit nervous*) I swear to you, Father, that I am
as surprised as you are. I didn't do anything to invite—

CHARVET: (*A beat*) Well, you know...even so... In
the United States such a visit would be completely
natural... So go ahead, Henri. Go and receive her in the
small salon.

(HENRI *exits.*)

CHARVET: Was that wrong?

HENRIETTE: No. After all, it's better that they meet here than among strangers. (*Making an effort*) And why shouldn't we receive her also? Come on, Father, let's go and bring them in here.

CHARVET: You think so?

HENRIETTE: Yes.

(CHARVET *crosses to the door on the left and pauses a moment.* HENRIETTE *stiffens her spine, sighs, and crosses after him. But then they back up into the room as* HENRI *enters with* NELLIE, *who wears a Red Cross nurse's uniform.*)

CHARVET: Mademoiselle, my son has told us about your devotion in caring for the wounded alongside him. (*To* HENRI) Henri, will you introduce us?

HENRI: Father, I have the honor to present Miss Nellie Brown of the American Red Cross. She's been awarded France's Croix de Guerre.

CHARVET: Very happy to meet you, mademoiselle.

NELLIE: (*Not shy*) Monsieur, it's a pleasure. (*Taking a step toward* HENRIETTE) Mademoiselle Henriette, your brother has told me all about you. I feel like I love you already. I hope soon you'll love me too.

HENRIETTE: (*Not cold, but not enthusiastic*) I will try, mademoiselle.

(*And nobody knows what else to say. They stand in place as the curtain falls.*)

END OF ACT ONE

ACT TWO

(A terrace behind CHARVET'*s chateau. Summer.* HENRI *and* NELLIE *are on stage. She wears a charming summer dress.)*

HENRI: …You got me appointed to a position!?

NELLIE: *(Cheerfully)* A done deal. They gave me complete authority.

HENRI: *(Tentative)* It can't be all that done.

NELLIE: But it is!

HENRI: But no.

NELLIE: We've talked so often about the settlement house—you understand everything about it. I even told you right before I went home: "What we need now for our low-income people and for our orphans in Chicago is a young French doctor, tested, prepared, speaking English… You, for example."

(He tries to interrupt.)

Wait, wait. And I asked you, "Would you want to come with me?" Let me finish. And you answered: "With you, I would go to the very ends of the earth?"

HENRI: But to Chicago?

NELLIE: Didn't you say "to the ends of the earth"?

HENRI: Yes, in a way. But Nellie—from saying that to a position in Chicago—

NELLIE: So often we've talked about this great work that my mother and I do. It's my life's work. *(Tender)* Henri, remember that evening when we talked about our lives, and we saw ourselves together always. Married. Helping the less fortunate, tending those who suffer?

HENRI: *(Overcome by the memory)* Yes, I remember.

NELLIE: You see! Back in Chicago when I said that I was going to marry a young doctor from Paris, they were so excited. I had to promise to bring you there as soon as possible. Of course, if I had my way, we'd have our wedding there too.

HENRI: Oh! But Nellie…

NELLIE: It's okay. We'll have it here.

HENRI: You know I have to complete my thesis first.

NELLIE: We'll have our wedding the very next day after that. And then we'll leave on the very first boat.

HENRI: You are incorrigible!

NELLIE: *(Coyly)* Are you trying to back out of marrying me?

HENRI: You sorceress!

NELLIE: Besides, it's too late now.

HENRI: Too late! What—

NELLIE: Yes. Do you remember what I told you when you met me at the station?

HENRI: That you love me.

NELLIE: And then?

HENRI: That you love me.

NELLIE: You heard that part. But then I said: "They are waiting for us in Chicago." And you said, "Anything you want". Is that so?

HENRI: Well, yes, but… Can I refuse you anything?

NELLIE: So I cabled right away. And I've already got a response. *(She fumbles in her bag and hands him a telegram.)* Look at this!

HENRI: *(A glance at the telegram)* This is crazy!

NELLIE: What's crazy?

HENRI: *(Reading)* "To Doctor Henri Charvet of the Paris Academy of Medicine."

NELLIE: So? Didn't you tell me you have a residency in Paris at the Academy of Medicine?

HENRI: At the *School* of Medicine!

NELLIE: *(Naively surprised)* School? Academy? What's the difference?

HENRI: I am not a doctor yet.

NELLIE: But you will be.

HENRI: *(Reading the telegram)* It's— But—! No. This is impossible. Nellie, I cannot accept this.

NELLIE: What's impossible? Why not?

HENRI: *(Reading)* "Please cable dollar estimate for construction of hospital, laboratory, surgical operating room, and microbiological research center." I'm not a surgeon! I'm not a microbiologist!

NELLIE: What we have here is a simple misunderstanding. Give me the telegram and I'll answer it.

HENRI: They need to know the truth!

NELLIE: Don't worry.

HENRI: You have to cancel this business! Can't you accept me as I am? As we planned when we got engaged. It's a beautiful life—the life of a country doctor in France. It's a life of total devotion, of happiness from knowing that you're doing good. Treating neighbors whose health is in your hands and they trust you. And the doctor's wife has a role in it.

NELLIE: Yes, you showed me that, and I saw the romance of it. But then on my visit home, my own vision of a future came back to me. I came to France for a great cause, and now that war-time mission is completed. At home I could see my larger purpose in life. I saw how much they need me there—the laborers who can no longer labor, the young women we rescue from the shame of their condition, the children we save from beggary and crime. Not to be there for them felt wrong.

HENRI: And what if I feel the same about being here?

NELLIE: Can you say that?

HENRI: Nellie, it's as if you're asking me to commit a crime.

NELLIE: *(Laughing)* A crime! To leave your father and sister to get married! You French are so quaint!

HENRI: Isn't it the same for you? You returned home to see your mother.

NELLIE: Not really. It was to revisit the settlement house.

HENRI: The settlement house got along without you for the whole year while you were in France. You have colleagues who can carry on without you. If they really want a French doctor, they can get someone other than me.

NELLIE: But it's all decided. You promised.

HENRI: In French? Not a promise, no. In English? Tentative consent, maybe. Or I simply couldn't refuse you. That's it. When you speak, I hear the music of your voice, but the sense of the words not so much.

When I'm with you, I can't think things over. I must have said yes, but—perhaps I thought I was accepting something that would never come about. Now that it's looming in front of me, I'm having second thoughts. Please don't say anything about this to my father and sister. It would hurt them so much.

NELLIE: *(Gravely)* I can be sure of one thing, Henri. It's that I must return to Chicago. You decide whether you will come with me.

HENRI: You say that so calmly! Is it so easy for you to imagine a complete break from me?

NELLIE: Love is love, but it's not *amour*. Here, under French skies, you think the world revolves around *l'amour*. My heart is full of—my attraction to you. There's respect and admiration, and—imagining you as my husband. But my happiness is in my life plan— with you or without you. Henri, you must face it. I will return to Chicago.

HENRI: *(A beat)* Then I am going to Chicago.

(HENRI waits for NELLIE's positive reaction, but none is forthcoming.)

HENRI: Still I must ask you not to say anything to my father or Henriette before I have time to prepare them myself. This will not be easy. Can you do this? Out of respect for him, out of friendship for her, and out of love for me? Let's not say anything yet. We can hold off until you return from your trip to England.

NELLIE: You know I'll be there for two weeks.

HENRI: All the more reason to wait. Let's be as we were during those three months last spring until you left for the United States. Then we'll marry and go on our honeymoon. We'll go to Chicago. And we will live there for as long as you love me.

NELLIE: That will be for the rest of my life. (*She moves toward the path from the terrace.*)

HENRI: You're going to the hospital now?

NELLIE: Yes, I brought back some gifts for the village children.

(HENRI *and* NELLIE *kiss lovingly, then she exits.*)

HENRI: Until soon…

(HENRIETTE *enters. She looks more serene and rested than she was at the time of* HENRI's *return. She goes to sit at the little garden table, and he sits opposite her. She reaches her hands toward him and looks lovingly at him.*)

HENRIETTE: You do look happy!

HENRI: Well, you yourself don't seem too unhappy.

HENRIETTE: Because you are here! Because you've found the love of your life! Because you love me and she loves me too!

HENRI: My sweet Henriette! Who could not love you!… But I must say, mademoiselle, my delightful sister, you are looking especially pretty today. I like your dress.

HENRIETTE: You recognize it? It's the one Nellie had made for me in Paris. I've been afraid to wear it. So she asked me if I don't like it. And that's why I decided to put it on today. Is it too much? I mean, is it wrong for…?

HENRI: Too much what? Wrong for what?

HENRIETTE: For my age?

HENRI: You look like a girl of twenty.

HENRIETTE: Flattery!

HENRI: Are you afraid of looking pretty?

HENRIETTE: (*Almost serious*) Perhaps… (*Laughing*) But it was so clever of her!

HENRI: Who?

HENRIETTE: Nellie. Without saying anything to me, she took my measurements from one of my regular dresses, and when she stopped in Paris on her way back to America, she ordered the dress. Then she picked it up on her way back here. You know, I think she wants to jolt me out of my spinster frame of mind! Now I'll tell you a little secret… This morning, as I was coming down the stairs, I caught sight of myself in the mirror, and I couldn't help thinking "That's me— looking good. That person in the mirror can't be thirty-two years old!" *(She laughs.)* Of course, I can't dress like this every day. *(She gazes admiringly at him.)* And now I'm thinking I haven't looked enough at you. My little brother all grown up! I see you as the man you are, the doctor, the married doctor you will be. It's what I promised Mama when she was dying. And it's coming true. And now I can get old!

HENRI: Henriette!

HENRIETTE: Can you believe it? That first day last spring when Nellie came—wearing her nurse's uniform… If anyone had told me then that we would so quickly call each other "dear sister" when we write to each other, I could not have believed it. But soon we could see her great, generous soul! I think I loved her from that evening when she spoke to us about her community home for the poor, and all the problems of her American city, and what she had done to help. She was so beautiful. She radiated bountiful energy. Do you remember?

HENRI: Yes…

HENRIETTE: And then, that whole month—all the little things she did for me! I wasn't used to that, but I let it happen. When she hugged me, I knew she was hugging you through me, but I loved that! She is honest. She has that American enthusiasm that knocks you back—yet it's combined with some actual common sense! Yes, common sense—so different from my stereotyped idea of American women.

HENRI: As different as you yourself are from her stereotyped idea of French women.

HENRIETTE: When I look at you, I see the same Henri, and yet so different from before.

HENRI: I've added a few years, you know.

HENRIETTE: Not for me. You'll always be my precious little brother.

HENRI: Henriette, can you understand—

HENRIETTE: What is it? You can tell me anything.

HENRI: (*Very tenderly*) Something I've been wanting to say to you. It's just that you still see me as a child, while everyone else sees me as I am now. So when you call me your "precious little brother" in front of strangers—well, I feel a bit embarrassed.

HENRIETTE: Was it Nellie who made you think that?

HENRI: In her country, family members don't get sentimental in front of others. You see what I mean?

HENRIETTE: Yes, of course. I'll be more careful.

HENRI: I haven't upset you, have I?

HENRIETTE: No, no, not at all.

HENRI: Because I could explain to her… It's how we are…

HENRIETTE: No, don't trouble her with it. But I do wonder—do you ever find her perhaps a bit… demanding?

HENRI: Demanding? Nellie?

HENRIETTE: Nellie. Oh, I know that in her country, young women expect to be admired. The women are very powerful there. But for us— It's something Father noticed. He said we need to be careful not to seem surprised—or how did he put it? —a little annoyed maybe, you might say, when she seems to expect people to let her order them around. It's hard to describe. There's something demanding… Pushy.

HENRI: True, yes, but that's what Americans are like.

HENRIETTE: But among us, you should be the one—

HENRI: It's a courtesy to accommodate the customs of those we take into our lives.

HENRIETTE: *(Smiling)* And there's something else. Father and I feel a little bit left out—sometimes even when you are there. Last evening, for example, when you and Nellie were speaking English. Usually you notice that we feel left out and you switch to French. But yesterday you and Nellie went on for so long—

HENRI: I beg your pardon. I really should have—We were in the middle of a literary discussion.

HENRIETTE: You both seemed so intense. What was the subject?

HENRI: It was about a poet.

HENRIETTE: Victor Hugo? Molière?

HENRI: An American poet. Walt Whitman. He's all about being American, and it's in the contradictions. Nellie has so many ideas about him and his writing. Her judgment is extraordinary. She brings a moral sensibility—

HENRIETTE: Enough! I believe you. But is this the best preparation for a country doctor's wife? Ever since she returned from Chicago, she seems less focused on it.

HENRI: There's plenty of time to think about that.

HENRIETTE: But you know, Doctor Bréançon is ready
to retire as soon as you can take over from him. He
brought it up again when I saw him yesterday, visiting
the little Bonain girl, little Louise.

HENRI: If I miss my chance with him, there will always
be another doctor to follow.

HENRIETTE: Henri! It could never be as convenient as
this chance!

HENRI: Nellie doesn't want us to be in such a hurry.

HENRIETTE: Nellie sees it her way, and we have our
way. Listen, Henri, I understand. She's young, she
might be nervous about fitting in here. If that worries
her, just remind her that I'm here to help out. I will
gladly handle any petty problems a young foreign
woman might have. You'll have a telephone at your
place. Whenever you or Nellie need anything, you call:
"Hello, hello, Henriette, can you come over?" And
quick as a wink, there I will be. I hope you weren't
worried that I might come and live with you. I would
never be that foolish or intruding. But I'll be ready
whenever you need a helping hand.

HENRI: A helping hand.

HENRIETTE: You'll still need a big sister sometimes.
You'll have Nellie for a wife, but she's so young. She
doesn't know you the way I know you. In fact, you are
still young—even after all your growing up in the war.
As a doctor, you'll have a motorcar.

HENRI: You've thought of everything!

HENRIETTE: Shouldn't my dream come true?

HENRI: It's a charming dream, and we have time to
think about it realistically. It's quite possible that Nellie
also has a dream.

HENRIETTE: But she must accept yours.

HENRI: That's our way of thinking.

(*A door from the house opens and we hear the voices of* SMITH *and* CHARVET.)

HENRI: (*Rises*) That's Captain Smith with Father.

HENRIETTE: Please stay.

HENRI: I can't. Captain Smith will be explaining his project again.

HENRIETTE: You might have some advice for him.

HENRI: No better than any advice you might give. I need to find Nellie in the village.

(HENRI *leaves the terrace by the path.* SMITH *and* CHARVET *enter.*)

CHARVET: Those are the trees you plan to take down?

SMITH: Yes, those. (*He sees* HENRIETTE *and makes a gesture of surprise.*) Oh, Mademoiselle Henriette, you look so pretty! (*He thinks better of his impulsive outburst.*) Pardon me. How are you this morning?

(HENRIETTE *and* SMITH *shake hands. She thanks him. He turns back to* CHARVET.)

SMITH: Yes, only those four.

HENRIETTE & CHARVET: Four trees!

SMITH: The pipeline goes here, in line with the boundary marker.

CHARVET: The boundary marker?

SMITH: Right there.

CHARVET: But that's the Chevalier Column—what you call a boundary marker.

HENRIETTE: You plan to take down our column too?

SMITH: Yes. It's not the tomb of some ancestor, is it?

CHARVET: No… We did some digging around and there's nothing under it. And yet it is shown on the very oldest maps we have. Simply listed as the Chevalier Column.

SMITH: So it has no purpose?

HENRIETTE: No…

SMITH: Then it doesn't matter if it's right there or nearby.

CHARVET: I guess not.

HENRIETTE: The very fact that we know nothing about the origin of such an ancient stone lends it a certain mysterious charm, don't you think?

SMITH: (*Gazing at* HENRIETTE) Bingo! That would not have crossed my mind. I get what you're saying, and there's something to it. But look, that little gazebo is on the same line—

CHARVET: The gazebo! Henriette, the gazebo, your mother's pavilion.

HENRIETTE: No, Captain Smith. It's useless to continue. There isn't a single corner in the whole park that isn't peopled with memories.

CHARVET: In 1793, there was a Charvet—

HENRIETTE: Let's stop right now, Captain Smith. My mother was there every day in summer.

SMITH: What about—instead of your ancestors—you consider your descendants! Respect for the past is fine, but the future must be created! Riches are sleeping under your neglected land. It's a crime against nature, against humanity—against France itself—to keep the land unproductive! This land could yield enough wheat or wine or whatever to support a hundred families, and you merely put a bunch of sheep on it! With the energy that could be generated here—energy you are missing out on—you could bring light to your local farmers. You could earn enough to build lighted homes for them in place of those unsanitary huts where they live now. You could spare them some of that back-breaking labor by investing in generators and tractors. (*To* HENRIETTE) Mademoiselle…Mademoiselle Henriette, when I was drawing up my plans, I visited each and every one of these farmers that I know you care about. I've learned how much you do for them— your gifts, your hands-on help, your sharing of the latest studies. I've been humbled to find out about all this. You, yes, all of you French people, you hide your virtues. I admit I used to have the wrong idea about the French. But after three years over here, well, I won't go on and on. But just when we think we understand you, that's when we don't understand you… But to get back to the subject, I've seen how you love those peasants. Don't you want to upgrade their lives? Replace their dark houses with lighted-up houses! Free them from relying on your charity!

HENRIETTE: I'm confused. I can try to find more ways to help them.

CHARVET: Captain Smith, this is all too much for us.

SMITH: Only four trees! Sacrifice them and a hundred other trees can grow.

CHARVET: And the Chevalier Column.

SMITH: We'll place it nearby.

CHARVET: And the little gazebo.

SMITH: We'll remove the sculptures and sell them in America.

CHARVET: And the lake. Will you send that to America also?

SMITH: The water in that lake will get a new lease on life. Right here.

HENRIETTE: And our memories?

SMITH: Your memories, Mademoiselle Henriette? *(Serious)* Let them fly away. They'll evaporate.

HENRIETTE: Memories don't evaporate.

SMITH: Build new ones.

HENRIETTE: With what?

SMITH: With projects! Productive projects!

CHARVET: Projects? I'm past the age for new projects.

SMITH: Why should you think that? As long as you have your health, you're always ripe for something new. In America we don't stop doing things just because the calendar says it's retirement age.

CHARVET: You have your ways. But this estate, these fields were handed down to me to pass on to my son. And if he has a daughter, they will be her dowry. An ancient heritage is a responsibility.

SMITH: Dowry. Heritage. Care to hear my opinion? Those are two strangleholds from the past that block the future. They've got to go. Like savings without interest, like guaranteed income. Killers of incentive!

CHARVET: You may be right. Henriette and I will confer.

SMITH: Thank you for hearing me out. I'll leave you for now. You understand the big picture, and you surely will see what's best for the future. Until soon.

(Farewell formalities. SMITH *is about to leave by the path when* PIERRE BONAIN *enters. He is a young laborer in his thirties.)*

PIERRE: Pardon me for intruding. Bonjour, Monsieur Charvet. Bonjour, Mademoiselle Henriette. I've been looking for you, Captain Smith. Remember me? Pierre Bonain. Marie's brother. And brother of your little friend Etienne. I looked for you at your place, and they said you were here. I've only got an hour for lunch, and this couldn't wait until tomorrow.

SMITH: What is it?

PIERRE: *(Joyfully)* The things that arrived today. All those things! So many things! I already knew the Americans were something different, but this! *(To* CHARVET*)* Did he tell you?

CHARVET: *(Bewildered)* No.

PIERRE: Things came from America! Captain Smith wrote to some Americans about us and they sent stuff for the kids and stuff for the grown-ups like Marie— and even me. We got—so much stuff—But best of all was a letter with it. A letter. It said they know all of us from Captain Smith's letters. They know the names of the little ones. They know that Etienne broke a window. *(Becomes serious)* And at the end, there was a prayer for my brothers who were killed. *(A beat)* We feel a great love for these Americans. Thank you, Captain Smith.

SMITH: *(Simple and straightforward)* Monsieur Pierre Bonain, the whole world owes friendship and gratitude to the people of France.

PIERRE: *(To* HENRIETTE*)* You know my little sister Louise, who was so sick?

HENRIETTE: How is she?

PIERRE: Ever since Monsieur Henri came to see her, she has been much better. Much better. She stood up in bed, and she was laughing.

HENRIETTE: Oh, I am so glad.

PIERRE: *(To* SMITH*)* If there is anything I can ever do for you—ever anything— Help you out in any small way. Give you a hand. Anything.

SMITH: Tell me again what you do, now that you're done soldiering.

PIERRE: I'm a mechanic.

SMITH: That's just what I need! A trustworthy worker for a new approach to work. I'll pay you double whatever you earn now. All I ask is that you adopt a system they're trying out in America that's increasing productivity three or four times over.

PIERRE: I'm your man.

SMITH: You understand the bargain. You follow the brand-new guidelines that I'll show you—for productivity.

PIERRE: What do I have to lose? Nothing. And especially to do it for you, Captain Smith. I'll come and see you tomorrow at your warehouse in the village.

SMITH: Let's go there together. *Toot sweet!*

PIERRE: *(Laughing) Tout de suite! Tout de suite!* You know that's not real French. That's an American invention.

(CHARVET *to* SMITH *who crossed to shake his hand:)*

CHARVET: Is that the Taylor system—Taylorism?—the work system you want to try?

SMITH: And make it work.

CHARVET: I wish you good luck. Until tomorrow then.

(PIERRE *and* SMITH *exit.)*

HENRIETTE: How shall we respond to Captain Smith's proposal? His sweeping plans make me nervous.

CHARVET: It would change our land and our heritage perhaps beyond recognition.

HENRIETTE: I agree. *(With emotion)* And yet, the way he spoke about life and the future!

(*Enter MONSIEUR* RINGEAU.)

RINGEAU: Bonjour, Monsieur Charvet. Bonjour, Mademoiselle Henriette.

CHARVET & HENRIETTE: Bonjour, Monsieur Ringeau.

RINGEAU: I stopped by so we could chat about various matters. And something about that Captain George Robert Smith, you know. It turns out that he's a good man, after all. It turns out that my son knows him!

HENRIETTE: Really?

RINGEAU: I haven't seen you since my son was discharged from the army hospital.

CHARVET: We were so relieved to hear that he arrived home.

RINGEAU: His battery fought in the Meuse-Argonne offensive along with the American brigade that Captain Smith was in.

HENRIETTE: The Argonne Forest. That's where he was wounded?

RINGEAU: Captain Smith, yes.

CHARVET: Yes.

RINGEAU: Because my son—his wound was at Verdun.… But the Americans, they were extraordinary. And Smith earned his medals. But that's not what I came to tell you. It was in September on the eve of the offensive, in some tiny village near the Argonne. Captain Smith found some poor old woman hiding near the ruins because she didn't want to be evacuated. Her hut had caved in around her. My son saw his friend Smith pick up the old woman in his arms and carry her behind the lines to safety. And Smith was saying over and over "don't be afraid." And then, to make her feel even better, he started calling her "mama". "Don't be afraid, mama." That is a remarkable story, isn't it?

HENRIETTE: He is a remarkable man.

RINGEAU: Well, the other day, I was with my son when he first saw Smith. I thought they were both going out of their minds. They were screaming and pounding their fists on each other. I heard "hi! hi! hi!" It sounded like a battle cry. And they danced together for two minutes nonstop. Hugging and jumping and they tried to get me to dance with them. Apparently this is what Americans do when they meet in the street.

CHARVET: They're young.

RINGEAU: That's just it, Monsieur Charvet. That's the word that describes the Americans: they are young. Ah, youth. It's beautiful. But I do have some serious matters for you. First of all, my inquiries about your future daughter-in-law are all positive. My colleague in Paris tells me that both her grandfathers were pastors of American churches. By American standards, her family is not wealthy, but it would be a rather hefty fortune for France. They are completely honorable. Her father worked at a factory and advanced into management and retired with a fine pension.

HENRIETTE: What about the purchase of Doctor Bréançon's patient list?

RINGEAU: About that. To my complete surprise, Miss Nellie Brown told me in absolute terms that they have other plans.

HENRIETTE: Other plans?

CHARVET: Did you insist?

RINGEAU: I insisted, and I saw that it was futile. She is a very strong-minded young woman. She has made a decision and her mind is closed to anything else.

(HENRIETTE *and* CHARVET *look at each other despairingly)*

Well, there's that. But I saved the good news for last.
I've just received a telegram from Captain Smith's
associate about the development of your property.
It affirms acceptance of a clause that Captain Smith
insisted that I add to your contract. They offer to pay
you, immediately upon your signature, sixty thousand
francs advance on future profits, to be deducted at ten
thousand francs over five years, only after you begin
seeing a profit greater than this figure.

HENRIETTE: Sixty thousand francs right away?

RINGEAU: It's iron-clad.

(HENRIETTE *and* CHARVET *look at each other.*)

HENRIETTE: Captain Smith would pay this out
immediately?

RINGEAU: The money is already held in account, in my
bank.

HENRIETTE: Father, we have to take it.

CHARVET: For Henri?

HENRIETTE: Yes. Otherwise how could we manage? *(To*
RINGEAU*)* Monsieur Ringeau, we accept.

RINGEAU: *(Shaking hands with* HENRIETTE*)* I congratulate
you, mademoiselle, and I am happy for you.

CHARVET: You wish this, Henriette?

HENRIETTE: Yes, Father. Will you go with Monsieur
Ringeau to sign for it?

CHARVET: *(To* RINGEAU*)* We can go this way. I'll walk
with you to your office.

(They exit. HENRIETTE *alone looks around. She sees* HENRI
and NELLIE *walking upstage, wrapped in each other's arms,
about to move out of sight.)*

HENRIETTE: *(Calling out)* Henri! Can you come over
here?

(HENRI *and* NELLIE *enter.*)

HENRI: I didn't see you there.

HENRIETTE: They say love is blind.

NELLIE: Hello again!

HENRIETTE: And how are all the little ones in the village?

NELLIE: Just look at these letters. We're connecting the children to so-called "godparents" in America and had them write letters for us to forward. They are absolutely charming. Oh, Henriette, there is something in the atmosphere of your beautiful country—a sweetness maybe. An kind of elegance in the expression of feelings. You see it in all these letters. These little boys and girls have few advantages, but they find the words.

HENRIETTE: It means a lot that you tell me that, Nellie.

NELLIE: Tomorrow Henri and I will read them to our friends at Is-sur-Tille.

HENRIETTE: *(Gently)* Oh, not tomorrow. *(To* HENRI*)* You know, Henri, we agreed…

HENRI: What did we agree on?

HENRIETTE: To visit the Dumesnils. *(To* NELLIE*)* These are old friends of the family.

HENRI: *(Not enthusiastic)* Oh, yes, I forgot!

HENRIETTE: We really are obliged—

HENRI: You can make my excuses.

HENRIETTE: You're saying—

NELLIE: We have plans.

HENRIETTE: *(To* HENRI*)* You promised me.

HENRI: Well, yes, but Nellie didn't know about it, and she arranged the meeting tomorrow with our committee for the orphans.

HENRIETTE: Nellie might have the kindness to inform us a bit in advance when she is going to claim your time.

NELLIE: They just informed us yesterday.

HENRIETTE: You could have declined such a late invitation.

NELLIE: I'm sorry we can't rearrange our schedule for you, Henriette.

HENRIETTE: *(Making an effort not to show her irritation)* Very well. In future, please do keep me informed. *(A beat)* How will you go? In a motorcar?

HENRI: Yes.

HENRIETTE: I'm thinking that the summer weather is changeable. You ought to take a coat, Henri. In case you return late. I'll get out your coat for you.

(During the foregoing, NELLIE has focused on sorting through the letters, with an occasional chuckle.)

HENRI: *(Searching in his pockets)* As you wish.

HENRIETTE: What are you looking for? Cigarettes? There are some in the gazebo. *(She exits toward the gazebo.)*

NELLIE: Here are your cigarettes. And I have your lighter too. You left them on the table after lunch.

(NELLIE gives HENRI the cigarettes and lighter while she goes back to reading the letters. HENRIETTE returns, carrying a box of cigarettes. She sees that HENRI is taken care of and puts down the box.)

HENRIETTE: *(Archly)* You are well provided. Whereas I don't smoke.

NELLIE: *(Sweetly)* Sorry, Henriette. I don't smoke either, but I rescued Henri's cigarettes and lighter when he forgot them.

HENRIETTE: Fine, fine. I apologize.

NELLIE: *(Simple, straightforward)* Henri, would you leave us for a bit? Henriette and I need to talk.

HENRI: *(Attempt at conciliation)* Nellie…

NELLIE: Go on, go on.

(HENRI *exits.)*

NELLIE: *(Loyal)* From the beginning, Henri told me so many wonderful things about you, Henriette. And yet—before I met you—I couldn't help wondering if you might be a bitter old maid with a dried-up heart. I intended to keep you at arm's length.

HENRIETTE: *(Sadly)* As you wish.

NELLIE: But now I do want you to like me.

HENRIETTE: Friendship doesn't happen because you say so.

NELLIE: It's earned, is that it?

HENRIETTE: That's it.

NELLIE: You led me to think I had earned your friendship, Henriette, and I was trying to be worthy of it.

HENRIETTE: Perhaps.

NELLIE: You even said one day that I was like a sister to you.

HENRIETTE: That's true.

NELLIE: You wouldn't still say that now?

HENRIETTE: Please. I'm having a hard time.

NELLIE: I think this is exactly the right time for the two of us to clear the air.

HENRIETTE: Think of Henri. He doesn't know anything of our differences.

NELLIE: He's the one who advised me to talk with you.

HENRIETTE: Well, then—

NELLIE: *(Without the slightest hostility, but also without tenderness)* Dear Henriette, have I done anything to offend you?

HENRIETTE: No.

NELLIE: Then why is it no longer the same between us?

HENRIETTE: It's my fault.

NELLIE: You've given yourself so generously to your brother his whole life. And now you are no longer the only one to look after him.

HENRIETTE: Perhaps. Yes, maybe.

NELLIE: *(Friendly but not affectionately)* Henriette, we mustn't let that come between us. Please don't hold a grudge.

HENRIETTE: No, of course not!

NELLIE: It's the most natural thing in the world. Henri is getting married. Already he has ties with people outside his family. This is the way of life. The Bible says, "You will leave your father and your mother…" Of course, it's tough when the family dynamic changes, but it has to happen. Back in the States we don't make such a big deal of it. A guy goes and gets married. Fine, life goes on. But here in France, your sentimental ways overshadow the practical considerations.

HENRIETTE: *(As if explaining)* I'm French.

NELLIE: An attractive French woman! But don't you see…those French feelings could carry us in opposite directions?

HENRIETTE: *(Coldly)* Everything you say is based in reason—the opposite of sentiment! Yes, I know I must adapt to new conditions. But those conditions are tearing me apart. *(More emotional)* Haven't you noticed anything? All those awkward…no, painful…

NELLIE: Awkward? Painful? Tell me.

HENRIETTE: What's the use?

NELLIE: What's the use? Well, so it doesn't happen again! You have to tell me.

HENRIETTE: Just now, when Henri left us. You dismissed him as if he were your chauffeur. And you often speak to him in that tone. Even if you do talk that way to gentlemen in your country, you could be a bit more thoughtful in the way you treat us—now that you are going to be living in France.

(NELLIE *makes a slight movement.* HENRIETTE *stops talking.)*

NELLIE: Go on.

HENRIETTE: *(Vaguely worried)* I've finished.

NELLIE: You want me to address Henri as if he's the boss?

HENRIETTE: Just try to understand my feelings—my humiliation—when I never wanted anything but to take care of Henri, and then to see you treat him as a servant? Sometimes you summon him to your side and it seems you just want to show your power over him, as if you possess him. Before you left, it wasn't as bad. But since you came back, it's out of bounds. It's the cruelty of a bully! a tyrant!

NELLIE: Bully? Tyrant? Incredible! You dare to see bullying in me, when you— Well, my "bullying" is only superficial, but yours is deep—entrenched. Mine, if it exists, is about nothing. Your tyranny aims to reign over his heart, his mind, his future, everything! You are his emotional jailer and you want to keep him locked up.

HENRIETTE: He wouldn't say such things to you.

NELLIE: You're wrong. There is so much more to Henri than you imagine. He loves you and he's grateful to you. Yes, he loves you. But let me repeat a thing he said about you: "The way she treats me—it's like a smothering kindness and I can't get a break from it."

HENRIETTE: Henri said that?

NELLIE: Yes, he did. And I've seen that it's true! You treat him as if he were still five years old. You dominate his days down to the tiniest details. But you make him feel stupid with your never-ending mothering and smothering.

HENRIETTE: Why didn't he tell me? He should have told me and not someone I—

NELLIE: Someone you detest. Yes, Henriette, you detest me and I can see it in your eyes.

HENRIETTE: I tried so hard to like you. But I've lived only for him. Since we were children. I gave my life to him. We were two orphans and we found the whole world in each other. But now, if he prefers you over me, if he confides in you instead of me... If I was possessive... Loving him was possessive? ...You said smothering. Emotional jail. *(A torrent of tears)* If that's true, I'm nothing now. If I were dead he would miss me. But since I'm living and I'm here, he runs away from me! It's all your doing. You wanted him all for yourself! You did everything to take him away from me. You came and ruined everything. You know nothing about the way we live. You even told me one day "I never cry".

NELLIE: It's true. I never cry.

HENRIETTE: I don't envy you that in the least. I do cry. I weep because I've lost a brother who loved me. For twenty-six years, caring for him has been everything to me. Then you, a year ago, you didn't even know he existed. He didn't know you existed. Then you came along—and because you are beautiful—you could destroy everything. It's no wonder I can't love you. If you cared about his family background, you would have seen my distress. You would have softened the way you tore him away from me. But no. You wanted to hurt me.

NELLIE: That's not true.

HENRIETTE: Not true? Oh, I overheard you. I don't eavesdrop, but I did hear you making fun of me. To him!

NELLIE: I have not made fun of you, Henriette.

HENRIETTE: You did! Down by the gazebo. You were belittling my way of dressing, the way I do my hair. Maybe I do look like a ridiculous spinster and that's why you sent me this dress. This dress. I put it on today to please you. This dress! From you! From you! *(She tears the lace off the dress.)*

NELLIE: Get a grip on yourself! Forgive me. Come on, let go of the lace. Calm down. I do see how much I've made you suffer. I am so very sorry for that. Stop and think. What really upsets you is that Henri is getting married—not that I am the one who's marrying him. You would have hated any woman who got engaged to him.

HENRIETTE: Oh, I don't know. I don't know.

NELLIE: He loves me. Do you really wish he didn't love me?

HENRIETTE: Oh, God, let him love you! Let him love you—since it makes him happy. What will he say when he sees me like this? Please don't tell him.

NELLIE: I promise I won't. Just a moment.

(NELLIE *gets her bag and takes out a small sewing kit to re-attach the lace on* HENRIETTE's *dress while they talk.* HENRIETTE *does not resist.*)

You seem overwrought, my friend. What can we do when things are beyond our control? Nothing. Unless you forbid our marriage. Is that what you want to do?

HENRIETTE: *(In a weak and sorrowful voice)* No, Nellie, you know I wouldn't do that.

NELLIE: Then you have to accept a situation you can't control.

HENRIETTE: I accept it. But don't take him away completely all at once. You have his love, leave me his affection.

NELLIE: That's all I ask too. *(Having finished the repair)* There. The torn part doesn't show. See how I made a tiny pleat to hide it.

HENRIETTE: Thank you. Nellie, I see that I was wrong. I will do my best to make you forget anything I've said that was unjust. I am really not a bad person.

NELLIE: Nor am I a bad person.

HENRIETTE: I know that. Everything you've done for the poor in your country and for the wounded here. I won't forget it. Let me embrace you.

NELLIE: *(Giving in to her like a child)* Yes, let's embrace. *(A kiss lacking tenderness but honest)* Only you must try to be reasonable, not give way to feelings.

HENRIETTE: It weighed so heavily on my heart.

NELLIE: There is something endearing about your French temperament. Almost funny. You know what would be fun! To cut short this engagement and move up the wedding date.

HENRIETTE: If you think so. Perhaps yes, that would be better.

NELLIE: When we see each other all the time, there's more chance of misunderstandings.

HENRIETTE: Perhaps so.

NELLIE: Remember how affectionately we wrote to each other while I was away?

HENRIETTE: Yes.

NELLIE: I hope we will continue doing that.

HENRIETTE: What? Write to each other? Are you leaving?

NELLIE: You know we'll take a honeymoon trip and then…

HENRIETTE: You're not both going to the United States?

NELLIE: Yes, we are. Didn't you know?

HENRIETTE: No.

NELLIE: I thought—

HENRIETTE: You won't come back! I see what you're doing! You'll leave and keep him over there.

NELLIE: Yes, Henri has been appointed doctor for our institution.

HENRIETTE: He agreed?

NELLIE: Yes.

HENRIETTE: He has to tell me. I won't believe it unless Henri tells me. At some point, there has to be a pull stronger than love.

NELLIE: Ask him.

HENRIETTE: How do I know you're not lying to me?

NELLIE: *(Irritated)* Calm down.

NELLIE *takes a paper from her bag and gives it to* HENRIETTE *to read.)*

NELLIE: Read this. It's the draft of the telegram I've just sent. You can see Henri's handwriting on it.

HENRIETTE: Not true! Not possible! He must have been out of his mind when he wrote that. Henri! Leaving! So far away! Abandoning us! No!

(NELLIE *calmly folds the paper and puts it back in her bag.)*

Now this! And you are so calm. You calculated it all and you think you've succeeded. But you're wrong. I know him. I know him longer and better than you! If he sent this telegram, he can send another… You think you've stolen him from us, but you're wrong. You are so conniving.

NELLIE: I swear I have not been conniving.

HENRIETTE: I see it now. You said you would stay here with us after your wedding, and when you said that, you knew already that you would take Henri away from us.

NELLIE: That's not true.

HENRIETTE: Just then. Just then. You sent a telegram without telling us. Isn't that lying?

NELLIE: I didn't lie.

HENRIETTE: He kept your plans secret as if he were hiding a naughty deed from me. And you did too! I wouldn't even know yet about your secret plot if you hadn't let it slip just now when you were trying to win me over.

NELLIE: Henriette, I am no more capable of lying than you are.

HENRIETTE: Lying must mean something different to you and me. You understand nothing about us! You will never understand our family life, our sentimental attachments, our respect for our parents, the bonds between father and son, sister and brother. For us they last our whole lives. The French family is something fine and strong that you can't imagine.

NELLIE: Yes, the French family truly is something special. And yes, it's different for us. But just now when you said I will "never understand" it, that was a moment of decision for me. I'm going to leave immediately and take Henri with me. I cannot and will not confine myself to your rigid, closed-off way of life. With your tradition-bound sentimentalism. I would suffocate here. Those walls covered with ancestral bric-a-brac are like a prison. They crush my spirit. I will not let myself be fenced in by your past. And that's why I'm taking Henri to the United States. I'm leaving tonight for London. In two weeks I'll be back for Henri.

HENRIETTE: He won't go! He won't go!

NELLIE: We'll see!

(NELLIE *exits.* HENRIETTE *slumps into a chair in a flood of tears.*)

HENRIETTE: Oh, God. He'll go with her!

(*Curtain*)

END OF ACT TWO

ACT THREE

(September 1919. The setting of ACT TWO has been transformed by the American development project. The trees in the background have been felled, allowing a flat vista, bereft of beauty. A huge shed masks part of the horizon. A telegraph pole stands upright on the terrace, and thick wires are strung from it in both directions. Part of the balustrade has been demolished. The cozy charm of the terrace is gone. On a large white-wood table are plans and tools.)

(At rise, CHARVET is alone on stage. A WORKER enters from outdoors.)

WORKER: Monsieur Charvet, I've come to alert you. The big oak—

CHARVET: Yes?

WORKER: We've finished with the branches. A few more strokes of the axe and it will topple. I'll get back to it. *(He exits.)*

CHARVET: Well… So.

(A moment later, HENRIETTE enters from the house.)

It's better for you not to be here, my child.

HENRIETTE: *(Looks toward the great oak, which she can see, but the audience cannot)* My poor trees! My great, beautiful oak! It has lived here so long! Men come and go, but it has stood superb. Look at them chopping away! It's going to fall—but no! It stands strong. And there they go again—chopping at its three centuries.

CHARVET: My poor dear Henriette! It's better not to watch.

HENRIETTE: *(Taking her father's hand)* I have to watch! My great oak. Those men are in such a hurry to get it over with—attacking it like an enemy. It's frightful how they go at it. And the American—look at him. He's working right alongside the others. Now they've stopped and they're moving away from the tree.

CHARVET: Yes, it's over. The oak will fall.

(A pause. CHARVET and HENRIETTE watch anxiously.)

HENRIETTE: Father, there it goes.

CHARVET: In all its majesty.

HENRIETTE: So slowly. As if it wants to rest on the earth.

(A loud crack is heard and then a low noise followed by more cracking.)

HENRIETTE: They've killed it.

CHARVET: All things die.

(HENRIETTE makes the sign of the cross. The triumphant shouts of the workers are heard.)

HENRIETTE: Why are the men so happy? It was beautiful. A beautiful, noble, ancient giant. Now it's as if a whole web of life is gone. The birds chose it for their nests. And we felt protected in the shade of its branches. Oh, Father, what memories it held for us!

CHARVET: See there, now that the dust is clearing. You can see their smokestack.

HENRIETTE: Their factory smokestack! It's ugly. It's brutal. And that is what we see now in place of the great oak that stretched out its branches like arms to protect us!

(A steam whistle sound comes from the factory.)

CHARVET: And now the cry of the beast.

HENRIETTE: That is what we will hear in the morning from now on—instead of the blackbirds and finches. Oh, Father, surely I was wrong to let this happen.

(HENRIETTE *sits on one of the steps down from the house. A different sound is heard in the distance.* CHARVET *crosses to investigate. At the broken balustrade he meets* SMITH *and they exchange a few words in lowered voices.*)

CHARVET: It's best that I go alone.

SMITH: *(Noticing* HENRIETTE'*s sad expression)* Monsieur Charvet, is Mademoiselle Henriette okay?

CHARVET: She's upset about the tree. Could you talk to her a bit? *(He exits.)*

SMITH: *(Approaching* HENRIETTE *in an upbeat way)* Hey there! Mademoiselle Henriette!

HENRIETTE: *(Slightly hostile)* See what you've done, Captain Smith. This was our peaceful little spot in the fresh air. From the time I was born, I looked out on a beautiful landscape here—until about a month ago. Now it's like a wasteland. The Chevalier Column lies there in pieces. That ugly shed. The balustrade— broken—where your diggers made an opening. And our wide-open blue sky pierced and wounded by that electric pole. The electric wires humming with plans to assassinate—

SMITH: It's a phase we have to get through to take us to a happier tomorrow.

HENRIETTE: It's not my happy tomorrow. Your open road to the factory can never give back my pleasure in the little path through the grass and bushes. Where my mother and I used to walk together. But you can never understand that!

SMITH: Do you really think I don't understand?

(HENRIETTE *looks even more discouraged.* SMITH *takes a lively tone.*)

Come on now, you're like the statue of tragedy I saw in a museum.

HENRIETTE: More like a ghostly survivor where she no longer belongs.

SMITH: Oh, boo, Mademoiselle Henriette! You are worth everything in the land of the living. Cheer up! This is no time for you to turn away from the new.

HENRIETTE: It's hard to let go of our past.

SMITH: All the same, over these months, I've noticed what strong stuff you're made of. I've noticed more about you than you can guess, and I know it's not the real you to be closed off to what life may bring. Think about your glorious French history. If people like Louis the Fourteenth or Lafayette... In fact, even way back in the 1500s—if people then—your ancestors—had your superstitions about the past, your chateau wouldn't even exist. Just think, it was built with the newest technology of their time. Am I right? Say something!

(HENRIETTE *looks at* SMITH, *but finds nothing to say.*)

SMITH: Okay. I get it. There's a French proverb: silence means consent. Yes, you will see that you can't forever prop things up beyond their time. Embalming the past is the opposite of life. Life is everything. We can make it better, more beautiful for all, not just for a few. But please don't think I'm working against you. Mademoiselle Henriette, you know... I would never want...I would be deeply down in the dumps if... Because... Well, because...

HENRIETTE: *(With a half-smile)* Because?

SMITH: *(Serious)* Because I want you to know that I love—that I want to understand—the French soul. *(A beat)* The others, well, maybe it doesn't mean as much.

But you… *(A beat)* Give us a week, and all this mess will be cleared up. Next spring, the charming spot you think you've lost will be all bountiful blossoms. In ten years or so there will be children playing here. And when they learn about what was here before, they will be grateful to you for giving them this place where their lives can expand. Mademoiselle Henriette, don't you believe in the future?

HENRIETTE: Once my brother leaves, my future is dead.

SMITH: Henri is leaving?

HENRIETTE: Yes.

SMITH: Well, so what if he does! It won't be his children playing here. It will be yours.

HENRIETTE: Mine?

SMITH: Of course, you'll get married…?

HENRIETTE: Me? Married!?!?

SMITH: Yes, you! It's a duty. You owe it to your ancestors. And to the future. Haven't you dreamed about being a mother of children on this same land?

HENRIETTE: Perhaps I once did. But the chance of that ever happening passed me by long ago.

SMITH: That's not how I see it.

(A beat)

HENRIETTE: *(Pulling herself together)* Captain Smith, I beg your pardon for keeping you away from your work. My petty problems don't amount to— And I know you have bigger things to worry about. Someone told me the workers have been getting restless.

(CHARVET *enters and crosses directly to* SMITH.)

CHARVET: Has there been any word at all from Le Havre?

SMITH: Nothing! I can't find out what's going on there.

CHARVET: Can you trust your associate there?

SMITH: I'm sure we'll hear soon.

CHARVET: I'm concerned about these men with time on their hands.

HENRIETTE: They don't have enough to do?

CHARVET: Captain Smith wanted to have them all ready to go as soon as the machines arrive from America. So he had them quit their old jobs. But the tractors are not here. They can't continue with the work.

HENRIETTE: And yet Captain Smith is paying them.

CHARVET: Yes. With money in their hands and nothing to do, they head to the tavern.

HENRIETTE: The war ended, but not our troubles. *(She exits into the house.)*

CHARVET: The men are unhappy about it. If Henri hadn't spoken to them—since they know him and like him—there's no telling what they might have got up to a while ago. Do you know who their ringleader is?

SMITH: No.

CHARVET: It's Pierre Bonain.

SMITH: Pierre!

CHARVET: I asked him to come and see me after their meeting. Because that factory whistle you heard was calling them to some sort of meeting. In my view, the method called Taylorism is inhuman—even though you pay them well for the greatest productivity in the shortest time. They don't like being ruled by a machine that tracks each movement relentlessly.

(Enter HENRI.)

CHARVET: What's the situation?

HENRI: They've calmed down. For the moment anyway.

SMITH: Are they still gathered at the factory?

HENRI: Yes.

SMITH: I'll go talk with them.

CHARVET: I'm not sure that's a good idea.

SMITH: Maybe not, but I'm responsible. *(He exits.)*

HENRI: I'm afraid they won't be very welcoming to Captain Smith.

CHARVET: Why not?

HENRI: They listened to me because they know me. Because some of them fought alongside me in the war.

CHARVET: Do they know that you plan to leave for the United States?

HENRI: No.

CHARVET: And you still plan to go?

HENRI: Of course I do.

CHARVET: I hear that Nellie has returned.

HENRI: Yes, she's at the hotel.

CHARVET: You're leaving tomorrow?

HENRI: Yes, tomorrow.

CHARVET: What will happen here after you go?

HENRI: Nobody is indispensable.

CHARVET: It's not that simple.

HENRI: What do you expect!

CHARVET: I respect your decisions. Yet it has seemed to me over the last week or so that you might be slightly hesitating. The visits to our relatives. And especially your long visit to the cemetery. And the affection they've shown you in homes all over the countryside.

How the tenants and the workers look up to you with such confidence. You know you have deep roots in this land. You know that?

HENRI: I made my decision. I've given my word.

CHARVET: So be it.

(*Enter* MARIE.)

MARIE: Monsieur Henri?

HENRI: What is it, Marie?

MARIE: Excuse me— It's important. I have to ask you. They say— Is it true? Are you going away to America?

HENRI: Yes.

MARIE: But what about my little sister?

HENRI: What is it?

MARIE: Louise will die if you go away, Monsieur Henri.

HENRI: Not at all. Doctor Bréançon will take good care of her.

MARIE: It's not the same.

HENRI: Of course it is. Doctor Bréançon is very wise and experienced.

MARIE: That's not what heals a delicate child. It's the love a doctor brings to it. Louise always begins to recover when she knows you are coming.

HENRI: She will soon forget about me.

MARIE: Maybe you might forget about her, but she—I don't dare tell her—it could take away her courage to live.

HENRI: Please understand, Marie, I have no choice. I've given my word.

MARIE: Well, then… May God be with you, Monsieur Henri.

HENRI: I'll try to see her one more time.

MARIE: I hope so. *(She exits.)*

HENRI: Marie, wait! I'll go with you now.

(CHARVET watches HENRI go off with MARIE. SMITH enters.)

SMITH: I couldn't get through to them, Monsieur Charvet. There's an atmosphere of hostility. The peasants called me some rather nasty names. They barred the entrance to their meeting room. It's a complete reversal of—good people that I've seen as friends—now they look away from me so as not to return my greeting. Not so long ago, they would welcome me with handshakes and smiles.

(CHARVET watches SMITH pace up and down. Near the balustrade, SMITH sees little Etienne, who is not visible to the audience. He calls out.)

SMITH: There's my friend Etienne! I see you. Etienne, come and let's play ball together. Etienne! *(A beat)* He's pretending not to hear me. *(Sad)* Even the children! *(He crosses to CHARVET and speaks seriously.)* Monsieur Charvet, are we Americans in danger of losing our friendship with the French? This special bond we've had ever since Lafayette?

CHARVET: Do you still feel friendly toward us?

SMITH: You're damned right, we do. It's a friendship tested by time, strengthened in war. Every American, every Frenchman, needs to hold tight to our bond of friendship. France is America's first and best friend.

CHARVET: Captain Smith, you are a man I like better every time I talk with you.

SMITH: This situation is awfully tough to take. Monsieur Charvet, I love France. I've tried to win the confidence of your neighbors. To think that I've failed in that simple reaching out! It's tough to see us losing the French affection that first welcomed us. On one ship after another, our soldiers are returning home without getting the chance to know the French people.

CHARVET: The saddest part, Captain Smith, is that the soldiers go home not understanding us while thinking they do understand us.

SMITH: What we've been through together… And yet we don't really know each other. You're right, that is a damned shame.

CHARVET: *(Gently)* You Americans come over here with certain high-flown expectations about us that we can't always live up to. At least not twenty-four hours a day, three hundred and sixty-five days a year.

(During this entire exchange, CHARVET *remains gracious, diplomatic, courteous. The more he seems to express reproaches to* SMITH, *the more he tries to be careful to avoid offense.)*

SMITH: I doubt it's so much a question of high expectations and terminal disillusionment as it is the little day-to-day misunderstandings. Our guys often feel exploited.

CHARVET: You mean, like the price of eggs.

SMITH: Yes, things like that.

CHARVET: It's their own doing.

SMITH: How's that?

CHARVET: The prices your "guys" complain about are the prices they set. From the beginning, nothing was ever too costly for them, and they had dollars to throw around everywhere. Buying up everything in the marketplace. So you mustn't reproach us for a situation that you Americans created for yourselves. And we suffered for it, but you didn't.

SMITH: That's going too far. Really!

CHARVET: Let's take it calmly. We have a big project underway together. Neither one of us wants to see it fall apart for the price of an omelet.

SMITH: You're right. But there is something else. We Americans want to be loved. Can you tell me, Monsieur Charvet, what's to prevent that? Good or bad, tell me.

CHARVET: We are—by comparison with you—generally reserved. We hold back. But you—how shall I say it? Your…

SMITH: Our energy?

CHARVET: It's more like your constant movement. Our peasants like their serene moments, but they see the Americans always in motion. *(Smiling)* It's true, isn't it, that you can't sit still. They say that Americans invented the rocking chair so they could keep moving even when they rest. Shall I go on?

SMITH: Please do.

(Enter PIERRE.*)*

PIERRE: You wanted to see me, Monsieur Charvet?

CHARVET: Yes, Pierre.

PIERRE: I came for you.

CHARVET: And here is Captain Smith.

PIERRE: Uh-hunh. *(Coldly)* Hello, Captain Smith.

SMITH: Hello, Pierre. What was decided in your meeting?

PIERRE: Our decisions—you will find out this evening.

SMITH: You used to take a more friendly tone with me, Pierre. *(A beat)* I haven't seen your family for a few days. How is the little girl doing?

PIERRE: Not good.

SMITH: Would your door be slammed in my face if I stopped by your place?

PIERRE: Uh…well… Not…

CHARVET: *(Conciliatory)* Pierre, think how your father would want you to talk to a visitor. Are you sure you know the whole story when you meet with the others?

PIERRE: *(Taking a more humble tone)* If I could be sure, would I stop to pray every time before I have to speak out?

CHARVET: It's no sin to speak and still get it wrong. It's part of learning. I don't have to tell you that I am your friend.

PIERRE: Yes, I know. My father's friend. A good friend to him. He had good feelings for you.

CHARVET: Captain Smith has shown your family much affection, hasn't he?

PIERRE: That was…

SMITH: So can you have a man-to-man conversation with me? I never did you any harm.

PIERRE: *(In a rush)* Don't hold it against me, Captain Smith. I can't go on with it. I tried—like a pig-headed fool, I tried again and again. Because I wanted to do right for you and keep my promise. But I just can't take it any more.

SMITH: You can't take what?

PIERRE: Being your machine's slave. Your system in the factory. Your machine telling us: "Economy of movement for maximum productivity." Your Taylorism telling us. Taylorism is Terrorism. Monsieur Charvet, you would be horrified to see what it does. You get in front of a machine and you have to obey it. Repeat the same movement over and over. Take a piece of metal, give it to the beast, take a piece of metal, give it to the beast, take a piece of metal, give it to the beast, and then another, and another, and another. No stopping. On and on and on. No stopping. If you miss one time, it clangs and makes a record of your mistake. I dream of hitting it with a hammer—I fought the Huns, but this is— If you need to scratch, if you blow your nose, if you think about anything—ding! the machine makes a record of it and reports you. Slavery run by a machine!

SMITH: Isn't it simpler than having a foreman tell you what to do?

PIERRE: No. The worst foreman, the most brutal foreman you can imagine, he still has distractions. Even the worst foreman has human time different from clock time. Sometimes he looks away and you have time to mutter a curse. But the machine—the nonstop machine—humiliates us.

SMITH: Humiliates!

PIERRE: Yes, you feel like what's-his-name Taylor is really wanting to invent a rod or a spring that can do the job better than a man. Captain Smith, I'm a man. I can't help thinking my own thoughts while I work, but the machine doesn't want that. I like you. But not your system. Forgive me. I just can't take it another day.

SMITH: You can't do what workers do in my country?

PIERRE: People are different in different places, Captain Smith. In France, see, workers like to understand what they're doing. They like to take their pride in doing a good job. When they finish one piece, they stop and look at it, and run their hands over it, and say to themselves that this is done right. Or maybe this could be even a little better. Not for the boss. For me, because I have my pride in my work. The rest of the team says the same as me. We're done with your methods.

SMITH: Our methods have been proven superior to yours.

PIERRE: (*A little irritated*) Then keep them for yourselves. After all, you can't tell a pear tree to suddenly start growing apples! Let each one do what it does best! That's my idea. Goodbye, Captain Smith.

SMITH: Goodbye then…

PIERRE: *Au revoir*, Monsieur Charvet.

CHARVET: *Au revoir*, Pierre.

(PIERRE *exits*)

CHARVET: Well, there you have it. The difference in national character or customs. You came in acting like a reformer, so sure of yourself, knowing what's good for everybody. And that attitude can put people off.

SMITH: Okay, I guess I can see that. And here's another analogy. We were like the firemen who came and put out a house fire and then made ourselves at home in the living room.

CHARVET: I'd add to that—

SMITH: What?

CHARVET: Then the fireman sent a bill to the insurance company. (*Serious*) Captain Smith, you had the right idea a while ago that each person should do his part to overcome misunderstandings. So… talk to your men. Let's think about this. You might tell them about the man I saw earlier, when he took down our great oak. The team had been sawing away all morning and they were almost worn out. When the last man comes along and doesn't know about all the work that the others did, he thinks he should be paid the same as them. France had been fighting, suffering, stretched to the limit, for three years before the Americans came over.

SMITH: It's true, there have been terrible mistakes of judgment.

CHARVET: On both sides, Captain Smith, on both sides.

SMITH: *(Animated)* But France can know one thing for absolute certain: Americans love France. I'm not talking about the military. We had a debt going back to General Lafayette and it was in our interest to pay it. But the real proof of love from the heart is how the women back home took up the cause. Rich or poor, American women all across the land were knitting socks and scarfs for the soldiers in the trenches. They collected money. They rolled bandages. They found a million ways to help, even back when our country was still neutral. Some even found ways to cross the ocean—risking torpedoes in the water so they could risk cannon fire on land—to help care for the orphans and homeless.

CHARVET: *(Very moved)* Yes, captain, yes, they did so much. I know it. I too saw it. Indeed, more than the sacrifices of your soldiers, the goodness of their mothers and sisters renewed those bonds of friendship between France and America. So let's deal with this misunderstanding of the moment. We can work it out if we don't let the resentments simmer and boil over.

SMITH: Together we can.

(HENRI *enters with a bicycle that he leans against the balustrade.)*

HENRI: Father, I met a man on the path just now who asked me to convey a message from Pierre Bonain. The workers and some of the farmers are at the factory, and they want to see you.

CHARVET: *(Hurrying to go there)* Coming with me, Smith?

SMITH: You bet.

CHARVET: Henri, did they seem overly excited?

HENRI: I don't think so. Apparently one of them, Victor Lamarre, was drunk, but they took him to the police station.

HENRIETTE: *(Entering from the house)* Father, they just telephoned from the factory—

CHARVET: Yes, I know. We are on our way. *(To* HENRI*)* You stay here.

*(*CHARVET *and* SMITH *exit.)*

HENRI: Henriette, I need to talk with you.

HENRIETTE: *(Her voice hard, trying to restrain her anger)* You've come to announce your departure. I know. Nellie has arrived.

HENRI: Yes.

HENRIETTE: What day?

HENRI: Tomorrow. The ship embarks from Le Havre on Saturday.

HENRIETTE: Yes, but she promised that the wedding could be here.

HENRI: She intended to hold to her promise.

HENRIETTE: No. You have been duped, little brother. She is more strong-willed than you suspect. She always intended to have the wedding in Chicago.

HENRI: I'm sure you're wrong—though I can't prove it.

HENRIETTE: I can't prove what I know either, so we'll leave it at that.

HENRI: As you wish.

HENRIETTE: Go then.

HENRI: I will. *(He starts to exit but turns back.)* No! No, no, no, Henriette, I can't leave you like that. I can handle your anger and reproaches, even your tears.

But this coldness, this pretended indifference—it's too much. In all honesty, there is only one thing you can reproach me for: that I plan my own life differently from what you fantasized.

HENRIETTE: I don't reproach you for that.

HENRI: Then what has brought this sudden change in you? Ever since I first opened my eyes in the cradle, I've seen nothing but tender care in your eyes. And now there's a hardness when you look at me. I need to know why.

HENRIETTE: I wasn't the one who started it.

HENRI: Is it because I'm marrying someone you didn't choose for me? Believe me, I know how much I owe you. You took the place of a mother to me and you made sacrifices for me. You did it all with complete good will. (*More tenderly*) This isn't right, Henriette. It's not worthy of you. My dear big sister, I might not see you for a year or two. Do you really want my parting memory to be this hardness in your face and voice? Even if I've done something wrong, how can we let it take away from our years of trust?

HENRIETTE: Stop, Henri! This hurts too much!

HENRI: Don't you think it hurts me too? I'm torn. Sometimes I don't know what I should do. But think about what you want. You want to keep me, because you're jealous.

HENRIETTE: Yes, I am jealous.

HENRI: In spite of all you've done for me, does that give you the right to control my life? It's true, you are a saint....

HENRIETTE: (*A beat, making an effort*) No, I am not a saint. You ask me to think about all this. Mon Dieu, that's all I do! I've discovered things about myself that are hard to admit—even to myself. I needed someone to love and protect—and there you were. It's true I wanted to keep you. Since you don't need me any longer, my life has no purpose. So now to face the truth: I loved you for myself, and it was always selfish.

HENRI: Oh, Henriette! Let's have no regrets…

HENRIETTE: You mustn't regret anything. I took payment from you for a debt you didn't owe.

HENRI: I owe you everything!

HENRIETTE: If you ever believed you owed me anything, you can rest easy. Your debt is paid—paid by the happiness I got from you. You even let me think well of myself. I took a lot of self-satisfied pride in what you saw as a sacrifice.

HENRI: You are much too hard on yourself!

HENRIETTE: There are so many women like me in France. In families everywhere, the daughters and sisters don't even question it. Of course we smooth the way for the heir to the title or fortune. What do these women get? A lonely old age. And maybe they seem a bit ridiculous. There are so many French women like me who cling and become possessive or shrewish.

HENRI: (*Taking her in his arms*) Henriette! Big sister. I love you. All my life I've loved you. Listen. If you ask it, I will stay. It makes me too sad to see you so unhappy. I'd be ashamed to leave.…

HENRIETTE: No. No. You must go, little one. Let me call you "my little one." I see that you do love me, and that is enough. You must go.

(HENRI *and* HENRIETTE *both weep while embracing. Enter* NELLIE, *wearing elegant travel clothes.*)

HENRIETTE: Here's your fiancée.

HENRI: Nellie!

NELLIE: What's the matter, Henri?

HENRIETTE: We were just saying farewell, Nellie. With all my heart I wish you every possible happiness. Abundant happiness.

NELLIE: Thank you, Henriette. Your words clearly come from the heart and that means everything to me.

HENRIETTE: *(Stepping away from them)* Now if you'll excuse me…Father and I will come and see you off at the station tomorrow. Tomorrow… *(She exits.)*

HENRI: Oh, Nellie, it would make me so happy if you wanted us to stay in France.

NELLIE: What's this?! Henriette finally accepts that we're going, and you ask us to stay?

HENRI: It's not for Henriette. It's for myself.

NELLIE: I don't understand.

HENRI: I love you, Nellie. I love you and will marry you. But I'm not happy. I have a feeling that I'm not doing my duty.

NELLIE: Whatever duties you leave behind here will be compensated by plenty of others over there.

HENRI: But the ones here are the more pressing. There is so much to do for our recovery from the war, and my country needs every one of its citizens.

NELLIE: One person's absence won't make the difference.

HENRI: Five years ago that would have been the excuse of a cowardly deserter.

NELLIE: You're not fleeing from any danger!

HENRI: Try to understand me, Nellie, with your great and generous soul. In America, everyone thinks the war is over. Yes, it is over for you. But for us, it's not. Winning the war doesn't end it. Dark forces attacked my mother, France. We saved her. But she's still gasping for breath, exhausted, wounded. It would be criminal for her children to abandon her in a ruined house. Oh, can you let me stay and tend her with you by my side?

NELLIE: You spent four years doing your duty to France!

HENRI: That doesn't give me the right to surrender now.

NELLIE: Don't you think we have problems in the States? Don't you think there are so many in distress, needing help with their daily struggles, just to get one step up the ladder to a better life? My mother created an amazing institution to deal with those problems. She and I are the heart and soul of it. They're waiting for me.

HENRI: You can show me that your duty lies there, but can you deny that mine is here? Isn't that so?

NELLIE: You're exaggerating your sense of duty.

HENRI: No…I see that neither one of us can be happy unless we are helping those in need. But, Nellie, your country is not ravaged as mine is. Your country didn't lose fifteen thousand of its children and see its land left scarred and barren. There's no comparison. And if only it were the material losses and needs! Nellie, my love, you love France. You proved it. You put your own life at risk a hundred times to care for our soldiers. I saw your tenderness as well as your courage. You became part of the whole French family, so I can let you in on a family secret. When I was traveling with Smith a couple weeks ago, I saw…I saw things I wish I had not seen, and especially not alongside a foreigner. I never imagined France could be—less than a year after our victory…. There's a change in spirit. So quickly forgetting what we had to do. The frantic, feverish partying. Forgetting about work. Forgetting even our honored dead…

NELLIE: In a way, it's understandable. After five years of danger, fears, terror—you don't overnight put down the rifle and settle back into the mundane job you left. Life wants its time back. People need to cram in a lot of living for the time they missed.

HENRI: But what comes next? We have to prepare a future. We need to re-awaken a sense of purpose. A new kind of mobilization. What a selfish pathetic creature I would be if I hadn't learned something from my four years of service! But I did learn how much I owe to the common people of our country. Nellie, with your powerful sense of loyalty, tell me: can I honestly turn to another country when my own country needs me so badly?

NELLIE: You want to remain in France?

HENRI: With you.

NELLIE: Or without me?

HENRI: Without you I would suffer so much. It would be very, very painful. But if I follow you to America, you would have only a man who's ashamed of himself.

NELLIE: You think it would be cowardly to come with me? I don't see that, but since you do believe it, it is true for you. Neither of us wants something like that to shadow our marriage.

HENRI: Please stay here.

NELLIE: But if my work means as much to me as yours does to you? If I were to feel less than myself if I give in to you?

HENRI: If…?

(*Long pause*)

NELLIE: We both see our best selves in choices that bring the pain of losing each other.

HENRI: We made such beautiful plans, and yet…

NELLIE: Yes, I did already live a beautiful future in my dreams. I can hold on to that.

HENRI: So will I. From the happiness we might have shared, there's a sweetness I'll never forget. And this separation…

NELLIE: I will keep you in my heart as long as I live!

HENRI: And you in my heart!

NELLIE: *(Moved)* Henri, no tears!

HENRI: No, no tears.

(Enter CHARVET *and* SMITH.*)*

NELLIE: Here's your father.

HENRI: Father, Nellie and I have talked. I'm staying in France.

CHARVET: Wonderful news! I always knew you would do what's right. Mademoiselle Nellie, you will stay with us?

NELLIE: I don't think so. I don't know.…

CHARVET: We'll talk later. Henri, things are heating up down there.

SMITH: They came to blows, and one is wounded.

CHARVET: I heard that some of them plan to meet at the police station at five o'clock—that's in ten minutes!—to storm the jail and liberate Victor Lamarre by force.

SMITH: I tried to talk to them, but they're so agitated. They wouldn't listen.

CHARVET: But they'll listen to you. Go and stop them from doing something stupid. Protect them from their own worst impulses. Jump on your bicycle. There are some from your regiment, so they trust you.

HENRI: *(Already at his bicycle on the other side of the balustrade)* Yes, father.

CHARVET: Henri, I'll be waiting down the hill if you can send a car.

*(*NELLIE *crosses toward the balustrade.)*

CHARVET: Where are you going, Nellie?

NELLIE: Someone is wounded. I'm a nurse.

CHARVET: Come with me then. Captain Smith, you stay here. *(Calls toward the house)* Henriette! *(To* SMITH*)* You get to tell her the good news.

*(*HENRIETTE *enters.)*

CHARVET: My child, Captain Smith has some good news for you. *(As he exits:)* Henri is staying here!

HENRIETTE: Henri staying here! Is it possible?

SMITH: He's staying in France.

HENRIETTE: And Nellie? Will she stay with us? Oh, I do hope so!

SMITH: I don't know about that…

HENRIETTE: But how did this happen?

SMITH: I don't know. I really don't know anything to tell you. But if it makes you happy? Does it?

HENRIETTE: So happy.

SMITH: Yes. *(A beat)* That chimney sure is ugly.

HENRIETTE: I agree.

SMITH: You know it's only temporary?

HENRIETTE: I'm glad of that.

SMITH: Did you really believe I would blight this beautiful land? There will be an electric station, but it will have no chimney. We'll plant shrubbery there, and the Chevalier Column will stand upright again, and the balustrade will be repaired as good as new. And this hideous post will be taken away, and the wires strung where they won't ruin the sky.

HENRIETTE: *(Softly)* Truly, truly?

SMITH: When you talked about the importance of memories, I got to thinking… *(He paces back and forth, tries to say something but hold back, then abruptly makes the decision)* Mademoiselle Henriette!

HENRIETTE: You frighten me!

SMITH: Are you absolutely sure you never want to marry?

HENRIETTE: What an odd question!

SMITH: Because if you could possibly reconsider—I mean, I know someone who would jump for joy to marry you.

HENRIETTE: Captain Smith, I'm too old for such a thing.

SMITH: Too old! It amazes me that you French put such stock into a date on a birth certificate! You let those numbers run your lives. A young woman says, "it's written down here that I'm thirty, so I've passed the age to think about marriage." Your age is not the number on the paper. It's what you carry on your face and in your heart. But enough of that. Let me shoot straight. You are an honest young woman and I'm an honest man. We're both old enough that we don't need to beat around the bush. I have every intention of spending the rest of my life in France. So will you marry me?

HENRIETTE: *(Flustered)* But…but…I never thought…

SMITH: Good. It's settled.

HENRIETTE: Settled?

SMITH: You just agreed to marry me and I am out of my mind with happiness!

HENRIETTE: But I didn't say yes.

SMITH: You didn't shut me up with a cry of outrage. You didn't tell me I'm crazy. You didn't tell me to take the first boat home. Clearly you saw the possibilities in me! You can make me the happiest man in the world. Take me!

HENRIETTE: It's true that I've always liked you a lot. And you have been such a comfort to me with all my anxieties. But to burden you with my age—

SMITH: Your age! Look at you! You have youthened ten years in the six months I've known you. You are meant to be a happy wife and mother.

HENRIETTE: You know I can't abandon my father.

SMITH: Who's talking about abandoning him?

HENRIETTE: And in any case, it would have been proper for you to ask him first.

SMITH: Oh, I already did that.

HENRIETTE: You did? But he would have come to me about it.

SMITH: He didn't have time. And then I couldn't wait to get happy!

HENRIETTE: This is happening so fast. I mean…

(*A noise from offstage.* HENRI *enters, his hand wrapped in a handkerchief.* CHARVET *is supporting him.* PIERRE BONAIN *supports him on the other side.* NELLIE *accompanies them.*)

HENRIETTE: Henri, you're wounded!

HENRI: A scratch on my little finger.

NELLIE: He prevented something that could have turned very ugly!

HENRI: Well, it would have been bad for that policeman.

PIERRE: It was that one idiot—

CHARVET: They were all riled up when we arrived. A bunch of rabblerousers wanted to invade the police station.

NELLIE: There was one guy throwing stones.

HENRI: *(Laughing)* And when I called for peace, I got two thrown in my direction.

CHARVET: *(Laughing)* And Henri bounded right over to the rock-thrower and hugged him!

NELLIE: *(Super excited)* Yes, Henri hugged him! I've never seen anything like it. He walked right into the middle of the riot and called people by their names, hugged, shook hands, this one, that one… And then there was the big guy trying to hit him— They hugged, and he lifted Henri off his feet and threw his head back and laughed. And there was some—you know, the kind of language soldiers use with each other. But it was affectionate. I couldn't believe what I was seeing. I was— But—oh, no—what's this? Am I crying?

(She weeps and laughs at the same time.)

I never cry. But these are tears. Does this mean I'm becoming French?!

CHARVET: Lucky France!

(Curtain)

END OF PLAY

www.ingramcontent.com/pod-product-compliance
Lightning Source LLC
Chambersburg PA
CBHW071350130726
47996CB00002B/872